WHAT OTHERS ARE SAYING ABOUT THIS BOOK

As Executive Director of a nonprofit that collects and shares first-hand refugee stories as a means of influencing policies and public perception, I was delightfully surprised at how Lisa Gerber's book made me think more carefully and deliberately about how our organization tells its own story. Filled with practical guidance, illustrated through poignant real-life examples, Gerber has written a practical guidebook that will empower organizations to engage more effectively with clients, donors and community members and she's done it in a way that feels like a candid and encouraging conversation with a close friend.

Kristen Smith Dayley, Executive Director,
Their Story is Our Story

This book unlocks the gold. Motivate, captivate, activate! I read it with an unexpected tension – a good tension – because the premise hits close to home. It's true, we all want to be intriguing. Have courage, find your why, add discipline and diligence to storytelling. The urgent balance of logic and heart is what so many of us seek to convey, especially for a cause that matters. Whether personally and professionally, trust happens when we cut through the noise. At every page, I bounced to the projects on my own plate and realized the guidance is dead-on.

Melissa DiBona, AVP of Legacy Projects, Operation Smile

When you write a book about storytelling, you'd better be a good storyteller. And Lisa Gerber is most definitely that. The reader learns not only from the process she describes, but also from the example she sets. Yet this book takes you beyond telling a good story to making sure you have a good story to tell. Every mission-driven leader has witnessed moments of impact and transformation — Lisa's work helps us to weave those golden threads into a coherent tapestry that will be both useful and beautiful. And like any fine storyteller, Lisa gives her readers a glimpse of who she is at her core, which leaves us wanting more. The good news is, there's more to be had when you work with her. Lisa's book is an example of a dynamic she describes within it: "I finally stood out by showing up as me — and people loved it."

Dr. Rebecca Sutherns, collaborative strategist and adaptability expert, CEO of Sage Solutions, author of Nimble: Off script but still on track (2019) and Sightline: Strategic plans that gather momentum not dust (2020)

An easy read but so much meat packed in every line! I literally just wrote up my walk fundraising story and now I need to go back to it. The advice is offered not in generalities but in real, concrete tips and resources that are easily accessible and will move your mission forward. Though I work daily with hematologists, I did not even consider an expert story and now I am excited to integrate that in our awareness plan. I also found myself taking notes to train my staff. Lisa also uses many analogies to her own life experiences that bring the tips and tricks of storytelling to life and make them understandable and relatable.

Michelle Kim, Esq., Executive Director, Hemophilia Foundation of Southern California

From So What? To So Funded!

FROM SO WHAT? TO SO FUNDED!

How nonprofits use
storytelling for impact and
change the world

LISA GERBER

Published by Lisa Gerber

First published in 2021 in Hope, Idaho, USA

Copyright © Lisa Gerber

www.bigleapcreative.com

Hope, Idaho, USA

The moral rights of the author have been asserted.

Every effort has been made to trace (and seek permission for the use of) the original source of material used within this book. Where the attempt has been unsuccessful, the publisher would be pleased to hear from the author to rectify any omission.

All inquiries should be made to the author.

Edited by Jenny Magee

Designed and typeset in Australia by BookPOD

Printed by Ingram Spark

ISBN: 979-8-9851385-0-4 (paperback)

ISBN: 979-8-9851385-1-1 (ebook)

To the change makers.

*"If you can get into the heart with a
story, you may not know at the time,
but people will go on thinking."*

- Jane Goodall, Time Magazine, October 2021

CONTENTS

ONCE UPON A TIME

"How can you change the world if you're failing miserably at changing hearts and minds?"

– Scott Harrison, Thirst (Harrison, 2018).

TAKE MY MONEY

In the summer of 2020, the COVID-19 pandemic forced us to cancel a client gala. It was a difficult decision as it was their largest annual fundraiser, and guests always look forward to the lakeside auction and dinner. But we couldn't risk the health of our community for the mission of the organization.

So they wondered: What do we do now? What will become of our organization? And what about our schools and the kids who benefit from the grants and programs we create?

If this sounds familiar, then you've probably had a similar problem. It's also likely that, at some point, situations outside your control have affected your organization's ability to achieve your mission.

Remarkably, when we sent out a notice cancelling the event, checks started coming in. We found comfort in messages that said, "We are sad you won't be having the event this year, but take my money anyway."

"Take my money anyway."

"Take my money anyway." Wow.

Wouldn't it be nice to create a culture of "take our money, anyway"? I had the pleasure of working with that organization for two years, creating a steady drip of storytelling to shift perception, drive awareness, and influence action. If we can do this with a small nonprofit with revenue under a million dollars, an endowment of less than two million and a staff of three (only two of whom are full time), then you can do the same with yours.

I've written this book for mission-driven leaders working hard to make their idea of change happen. You are a communications professional, a program director, a fundraiser, a policy advisor. You are a board member, a founder of a nonprofit, a volunteer. You are working to make change happen, and therefore, you are a leader.

You know storytelling is critical to your mission, but it's a lot easier said than done. You and your team are stretched thin and can't possibly add more to your plate. Maybe you don't know where to start, how to engage your team, or who should tell the stories. Some of you are telling stories, but they aren't driving results, and you can't understand why. Most importantly, you have dedicated your life to a cause you care about, and it's frustrating that you can't seem to articulate it in a way that gets others on board.

If that's you, then you are in the right place. I'll draw upon personal and client experiences and stories from the private and nonprofit sectors throughout the book. My intent is to inspire you with new ways of thinking and new ways of telling stories. I have attempted to keep it as simple as possible without adding a lot of busy work. I hope that, by the end, you will have developed and begun to implement a plan. My hope for you is that you will become more effective at using stories to get noticed. In doing so, you will get the resources you need to tell more stories, which will bring in more resources. The results will be so compelling, you and your team can't afford not to tell stories.

IT'S MORE THAN STORIES

The client who had to cancel the gala attributed their donors' "take my money" attitude to a steady cadence of storytelling over the years.

Over lunch, I suggested that it's not entirely the stories that got her there; the organization's backbone is the excellent work that she and her team do. But if you do all this good work and no one knows about it, were you really doing anything?

It's up to us to take all that activity and curate and package it into stories your audiences can latch onto. All so they can understand, remember and be informed enough to take action.

Think about who you regularly turn to for news. You have developed trust and a relationship with this person, even though they have no idea who you are. They have successfully scaled relationships by turning what's happening in the world into stories that you can understand and make informed decisions about. You don't have time to watch C-SPAN and read legislative bills. You don't have time to follow everything going on in the world, nor do you have access to do so. You rely on your news source for that.

I invite you to take on the role of news anchor and producer in your organization.

Your organization needs someone to curate and package all the great work you are doing into stories that your audience can understand and relate to – and trust. If you are memorable, they will talk about you and keep coming back. And they will take action – whether to volunteer, sign a petition, vote, or donate.

> We can all make the world a better place, one story at a time.

The work you do is what matters, but the story is the catalyst for change. A steady drip of storytelling elevates your organization to "take my money, anyway".

We can all make the world a better place, one story at a time.

WHERE IT ALL BEGAN

I was home for the holidays in the middle of my senior year in college when it occurred to me that in less than six months, I'd be out of college. I realized that no one would be telling me where to go or what to do for the first time in my life. I would soon be on my own.

And I didn't have a plan.

Apparently I lived in the moment during those college years – not sure how that happened; perhaps it's a question for another book. When I expressed my anxiety, Dad casually suggested I move to Colorado. We used to go there on family ski trips, and he knew how much I loved the place. Not one to argue with him (have a little respect, eh?), I followed his advice and enjoyed a life of skiing by day and waiting tables for the rich and famous at night.

After two years, a series of events, or shall we say signals, took me from Aspen to Seattle. It was time to put my college degree to work, and I like to pay close attention to signs and opportunities along the way through life. I landed in Seattle sight unseen, with a return ticket in my pocket. If I couldn't make it work, I'd go back to my hometown and figure out what was next. If I could make it work, I'd fly back to get the rest of my stuff and drive out.

Seattle did work out, and I eventually applied my degree in communications in urban development and revitalization. One morning, the company I worked for announced they had bought a ski resort in Idaho. How serendipitous. Even more so when the resort's marketing director left to get married, and they asked me to take the position. Life came full circle, and I was back in the mountains doing work I loved with skis hanging in my office.

A few years later, feeling restless for more challenging work, I took a month-long sabbatical to figure out what I wanted to do with my life. As I reflected on all the work I'd done, I realized that my favorite part was helping the media find stories for their audiences. Writing for a family-friendly magazine? That's one story. A foodie magazine? Another story. High adventure? My favorite.

Having been influenced by stories (who hasn't?), I knew this was what I wanted to do. So I returned to work with a proposal for my employer. I'd leave my position, start my own practice and handle the PR for the ski resort. They agreed to be my first client, and it was done.

On a rainy afternoon a few days later, I sat in the passenger seat of the car, forehead against the window, rain streaming down the glass, terrified. I worried that I was leaving a great (and the only) job for me in the community. What if it didn't work? What if I became destitute? This is such a big leap, I told myself.

TAKE A BIG LEAP

And on that day in July of 2004, Big Leap Creative was born. Since then, storytelling, as we know it, has evolved alongside the media and technology. We no longer rely on magazines, newspapers, and news outlets to tell our stories. Now that organizations can tell their stories directly to the world, there is enormous potential, great opportunity. There's so much work to be done.

> Now that organizations can tell their stories directly to the world, there is enormous potential, great opportunity.

My place in this world is helping people (like you) who have dedicated their work to meaningful change. Helping articulate your messages to get people to care about your thing amplifies my desire to make the world a better place – one story at a time.

HOW IT ALL FITS TOGETHER

This book draws on my twenty years of experience in the private and nonprofit sectors, both from personal and work perspectives, and the brands and organizations that fascinate me.

Rather than offering a twelve-step process to writing a great story, as some experts and books suggest, I want to inspire new ways of thinking. I believe it's not your storytelling skills that are lacking; it's your stories. You don't have to be a master storyteller; you just have to know which stories are the most meaningful at the right time.

When you tell more compelling stories, you become more effective at storytelling.

There is no linear process, so please bounce around and revisit each section as needed. Have fun, and be inspired.

Just as you will do in your storytelling, I've had to make many decisions about what to include and leave out of this book. In which order should things go to make it flow? Who will help me by editing, reading, and giving feedback? How will I publish and market the book? There are three stages to building a story, whether it's for an Instagram post, a blog or grant application, donor appeal, a speech, or a full-blown book.

Discover

What is your story? This is not an easy question because there are countless ways to respond and many different stories to tell. When I told you my story, I had to think about purpose first. What do I want the story to do? Will it matter to you? How will you relate to it? How can I use the story to build trust and understanding? This section is where we'll reflect upon what matters for your story. We'll ask good internal questions to determine the right stories and ask good external questions to discover those stories. I call this part Storylistening.

Distill

Once I had determined the basic material I wanted to include in my personal story, I started writing and then revised. We'll examine the questions and processes I put myself through to ensure the story matches the reader's needs. You'll learn how to structure everything you've collected. You'll also understand how different stories suit different objectives and how to make the hard choices of what to include and what to leave out. I call this part **Storycrafting**.

And finally:

Distribute

If you tell a great story and no one hears it, is it really that great? Getting your narrative out in the world is a big leap – that's when things get scary and make you vulnerable. You'll learn how to create momentum and leverage your stories to save time. This is **Storytelling**.

> If you tell a great story and no one hears it, is it really that great?

But first, let's explore how stories work.

THE SCIENCE OF STORY

I was two miles from the finish line of a trail race in the North Cascade Mountains, and my energy was beginning to flag. Two miles left feels like you're almost done, but no matter how you slice and dice it, two miles is still two miles. I could hear the crowd at the finish line off in the distance; their loud encouragement echoed up the quiet valley motivating me to carry on.

As I wound my way down the trail, weaving through the forest, the noise got closer. I rounded the corner onto a suspension bridge lined with spectators cheering and waving. My emotions began to bubble, and I quickly reminded myself that this wasn't the Olympic trials. Turning the corner into the finish chute, I was overwhelmed with the ruckus, yet I heard one quiet word through it all. "Honey". I knew that voice and turned to find my husband in the crowd, camera poised. I smiled and waved for the photo, then continued the final few yards to the finish.

Later, I wondered how Patrick was able to get my attention like that. He didn't yell or wave his arms; he just said, "Honey" in his low, familiar voice. He was no match for the noise of the crowd, yet he had no trouble cutting through, getting my attention, and influencing me to take action (smile for the camera). Wouldn't it be nice to achieve a similar level of trust and focus as organizations? How might we develop a similar bond with our audience?

It turns out there is a hormone that bonds people together. It's called oxytocin – often referred to as the Love Drug. In a nutshell, what happens is that part of the brain releases oxytocin when neurons are excited. What excites neurons? Things like hugs, sex, and connection with a loved one.

I have good news – organizations can trigger the release of oxytocin in our audience. And we can do so without sleeping with them! Something else that releases oxytocin? A good story.

That's right. A good story sustains attention, causes tension and anticipation. It produces empathy as we experience it and live vicariously through the characters. Familiarity affirms that it is OK to approach and to trust.

What's more, stories are emotional and personal and engage more of the brain. Facts and data use only the auditory cortex, while a story activates the motor, sensory and frontal cortices, making information easier to remember.

Once we get attention, create trust and empathy, and stay top of mind, we are more likely to motivate behavior and influence action.

Research by Network for Good found that fifty-six percent of 400 nonprofits reported an immediate increase in giving when they used better storytelling skills. What happened with the other forty-four percent? It was either too soon to tell, or they didn't know (Chase, n.d.). We'll talk about tracking outcomes later.

As you can see, your stories accomplish a variety of objectives. When used strategically, your stories take your audience on a journey. From never having heard of you, your stories do the hard work of moving them to being emotionally connected to you.

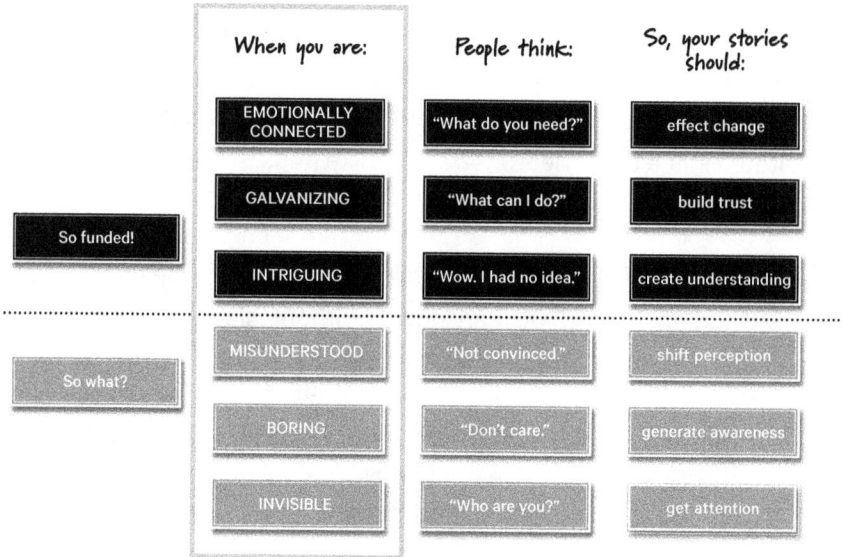

	When you are:	People think:	So, your stories should:
	EMOTIONALLY CONNECTED	"What do you need?"	effect change
So funded!	GALVANIZING	"What can I do?"	build trust
	INTRIGUING	"Wow. I had no idea."	create understanding
So what?	MISUNDERSTOOD	"Not convinced."	shift perception
	BORING	"Don't care."	generate awareness
	INVISIBLE	"Who are you?"	get attention

When done well, you've elevated your organization from So What? To So Funded! Let's find out how.

STORY WITH PURPOSE

It's helpful to understand how relationships build over time with your constituents. Instead of feeling overwhelmed by all the work you have in front of you, this section will help you identify your priorities.

THE SIX STATES OF STORY

Invisible

You are an unknown entity when starting out (either as an organization or in your storytelling journey). People don't know who you are or that you exist. It is hard to get anything done. At this stage, you simply want to get attention.

Boring

Facts and data are important, but they are dry and rather boring. I mean, when was the last time you sat down gripped with excitement, put your feet up, and opened up a book of facts and data? If your communications are boring, you won't cut through the noise with the usual arguments and appeals. You go unnoticed, and people don't know who you are. You can't get things done or fund programs because the right people don't know about you.

If you find yourself here, then your stories need to work hard to generate awareness. You are likely educating your audience about a problem or gap you meet, but they may not know it needs solving. Your job is to highlight the issue, share why it is a problem, why they should care, and why *you* are the organization to help fix it.

Misunderstood

You're known for something at this level, but it may not be what you want to be known for. Organizations are misunderstood when misinformation circulates, or an incident occurs. Your audience might not quite get what you do, or perhaps there is controversy around your cause or issue.

When this happens, your stories should focus on shifting perception. What can you tell that will get people to think differently about your cause or organization?

Intriguing

Once you get your audience to understand you, and they think, "Wow, I had no idea!", at that point, you have become intriguing, and they will follow you. Hopefully, they will subscribe to your email list and follow you on social channels. You can stay top of mind and be memorable.

Galvanizing

Being memorable and intriguing is nice, but we really want people to do something. Your stories drive action because you've galvanized them. They are showing up, volunteering, signing petitions, knocking on doors. You've worked hard to build trust, so people are willing to give one of their most precious assets: time.

Emotionally Connected

When you get to this stage, you've rallied a community that believes in you and wants to help you make change happen. They are emotionally connected, so you can cancel your largest fundraiser of the year, and they will still ask, "What do you need?"

WHERE ARE YOU?

As you think about where your organization sits on the ladder, keep in mind that you could be in all places at once, shifting up and down the ladder on any given day. You'll have audiences in various stages of their relationship with you. Your stories take less effort to drive action and raise funds when you rise above the dotted line. You are effecting change. Meanwhile, below the dotted line, you still work to make a case for your organization and your cause. It takes more effort and more time.

The people you want to reach may care about your thing, but they might not have heard of you yet. Regardless, they are like you and me, approaching the finish line, continually bombarded by cheering brands and organizations competing for our attention. At every minute, we make choices about where to give our time, attention, and money. And we get good at blocking out what does not serve us and tuning in to what does.

It took many years of developing trust and understanding for my husband to be able to cut through the noise and get my attention. (I told you this wasn't the quick and easy guide.)

It doesn't have to take that long for you. It won't take decades, but it will take time and effort – and heart.

WHAT EXACTLY IS STORY?

"You keep using that word. I do not think it means what you think it means."

– Inigo Montoya, The Princess Bride (Goldman, 1973).

It might be helpful to step back and explain what we mean by story. It's a very trendy word of late, one that gets thrown around so much that I fear we've begun to lose sight of what it really means.

According to the online Merriam-Webster Dictionary, a story is "an account of incidents or events; a statement regarding the facts pertinent to a situation in question" (Merriam-Webster, n.d.). In the context of a brand story, it's a narrative about your organization that comprises facts and incidents while inspiring an emotional reaction.

Alex Blumberg, the producer of This American Life and other radio news shows, defines a story as a narrative of events with a rising action that culminates with a turning point – it might be a moment of realization or a turnaround for the hero in the story – and a resolution (Abel & Glass, 2015).

Author Bernadette Jiwa says many things contribute, wittingly or not, to your brand story, from staff uniforms to customer experience (Jiwa, n.d.). Your story is more than what you and your staff say. It's the experience you offer, the events you create, the makeup of your board, donor communications, and the benefactor experience.

A story can be one sentence, one paragraph, or many pages. It can even be your mission statement (although most are not). It can be a paragraph in the overview of your grant report or the tagline on your home page. It's the video you use at public meetings, the end-of-year fundraising campaigns, and the assessment in your research report.

A photo or a graphic tells a story. We start to see that the word "story" is used loosely because it has many useful applications. The problem is that people often think they are telling a story when they are only offering a chronology of events. That is not a story.

When is a Story Not a Story?

Let's take a box of tea as an example – one in my kitchen pantry has "Our Story" written on the side. It says:

> The problem is that people often think they are telling a story when they are only offering a chronology of events. That is not a story.

Back in 1969, we started picking herbs from the fields and forests of the Rocky Mountains, and at that moment, we created America's very first herbal tea. Still blended in Boulder by our expert blendmaster, our uniquely delicious teas are made with the finest ingredients, passion, and inspiration.

It's a couple of sentences that talk about picking herbs in the mountains. Does something happen? Are you eagerly anticipating the ending? Would you tune in for the next paragraph? Does anyone care? Is it really a story? Our judges say, "No".

What about the following example? Nicole Grimm, a nurse practitioner at Woodlands Family and Community Medicine in Sandpoint, Idaho, gave a grant presentation on behalf of Bonner Partners in Care Clinic, where she volunteers. She introduced herself and the concept of the free clinic that serves those who fall in the insurance gap. These people either have super-high deductibles or can't afford insurance and opt for the tax penalty rather than the coverage. Nicole described the numbers of visitors to the clinic, those who fall in the gap and are underserved in the market, and explained the many services they provide.

And then she stopped and said, "Let me tell you a story about a young girl who confirmed exactly why I do what I do." Nicole described a teenage girl who worked at a local pizza place and came in for ongoing stomach pains. She had some tests done, but there appeared to be nothing wrong when she returned a week later to review her results.

Thinking that things weren't adding up, Nicole asked more questions. She learned that this girl had never consulted a doctor before. The only time she ate was at work because she couldn't afford to buy food. She suffered from anxiety, and she was hungry. As Nicole said, "Right here in my own town! I probably bought a pizza from her and didn't give her a second thought."

Nicole described how she connected this girl with resources to help her – the local food bank and mental health professionals. She said, "I can be as exhausted as ever from a full day at work, but when I show up for my volunteer shift at the clinic in the evening, I stay as late as needed. I will never turn anyone away. That is why I do what I do."

Is it a story? Did something happen? Did you get pulled in to hear if there is a happy ending? Did anyone care? Yes – to all of that.

That is a genuine story, and because of it, Bonner Partners in Care Clinic won the $10,000 grant that evening.

But there are good stories and bad stories. Why else would you avoid the crazy colleague going on about "themself" at the holiday party? You know, the one who traps you in a corner and bores you to tears about how he managed to resolve the storage issue in his Macbook Pro. Or the chatty neighbor you avoid by ducking down a different aisle at the grocery store – all because you don't want to hear about their latest gardening feats. Nothing is more painful than getting trapped by a boring storyteller telling bad stories because they are so hard to escape.

Escape isn't a problem for your audience. If you play the role of that crazy colleague going on and on about themselves or the chatty neighbor with nothing significant to say, your audience will easily scroll past and ignore you. They have plenty of other options for their time, attention, and resources.

And that bears the next question: What is a *good* story?

WHAT IS A GOOD STORY?

"A tale well told is nature's way of seducing us to pay attention to it."

– Lisa Cron, Wired for Story (Cron, 2012).

Movie producers are not phoning Nicole Grimm to purchase the rights to the story she told at the grant presentation. Does that mean hers wasn't a good story?

Quality, not Quantity

Check any book or movie reviews, and I challenge you to find a universally liked story. Ask your friends about their favorite Netflix series and let the debate commence.

No single story appeals to everyone. In fact, in our unending desire to create a story that everyone likes, we sacrifice our ability to be loved by a smaller group. A good story doesn't try to be something to everyone. You simply want to get people to care enough about your thing to make your idea of change happen.

Most of you are not trying to create a literary masterpiece or vying for the Pulitzer Prize in your storytelling efforts. A tale well told doesn't have to be stunning or poetically written. The substance of your story will shine without an MFA in creative writing.

> A great story gets you noticed, makes you memorable, and influences action.

In the context of nonprofit storytelling, a good story attracts the right people. A great story gets you noticed, makes you memorable, and influences action. Hypothetically, let's say you recount a story that everyone likes. What good is it if they don't remember you or do something with it? A story told to a room packed with people who did nothing would be unsuccessful – unless you aimed only to raise awareness. We'll talk about objectives and metrics in the next chapter, but for our purpose, what makes a story good is reaching the right people and moving them to action. Whether it's one person or a hundred doesn't matter.

Going viral is the lottery, building momentum is the strategy.

Your organization is complex, with many layers, many stories to tell, and many audiences to reach. Stories fail when we talk about what we think is important and not what matters to our audiences. We tend to lead with our mission, or 501(c)3 status, our new website, or how close we are to our funding goals. Our 25th anniversary? Yay! But other people don't really care about that stuff. It's not that those things are unimportant, but they don't form a compelling story that gets people excited and emotionally invested.

To be an effective storyteller, you have to tell an effective story.

Reflect on your journey from So What? to So Funded!, going from invisible to boring, misunderstood, intriguing, and galvanizing. To be emotionally connected, you have to move your audience on to the next stage. At each point, they will have different feelings about you that progress. They've never heard of you. They don't care about you. They aren't convinced. They start to get it. They ask, "What can I do?" And then they ask, "What do you need?"

> To be an effective storyteller, you have to tell an effective story.

Remember their needs before your own, and you've got them.

Your job is to know what questions are on their minds. You'll need to address them proactively before they are willing to take action. Your funders, volunteers, board members, and community members all have needs. They need to understand you, trust you, and remember you first. Then, and only then, will they do what *you* want.

A good story meets their need, and it's really awkward if you miss the mark. Just as most people wouldn't propose marriage on a first date, you wouldn't start a conversation with someone who hasn't heard of you with a big ask.

Matching the story to the need is just a fancy way of saying "having a conversation". And that's what storytelling is – engaging in a conversation with your audience.

THE SECRET WEAPON OF STORY

I talked about the science of story and how we can use it to move audiences from unconvinced to emotionally connected. A story can be as short as a sentence or photo, but something has to happen. There has to be some action. Matching it to your audience is key to building a community of people invested in helping you to achieve your mission.

Before you start the actual work of telling a story, it's helpful to understand the power it helps you wield. Forget about the science stuff – that was just to convince you that stories matter. I also shared a rather complex diagram mapping out where you are as an organization, what people think of you, and what your stories do. It's a helpful resource to return to, but I don't expect you to memorize it.

What I hope you'll hold on to is this. We want people to notice, understand, trust, remember and take action with us. Combined, these create a relationship that equates to an emotional connection.

People want evidence, so your data and statistics are important. The stories make an emotional connection and, therefore, your case. They remove the transactional nature from the relationship, making you the organization of choice. That's when they say, "what do you need?" instead of "who are you?"

The biggest pitfall is when we focus so heavily on what we want our stories to achieve (the gift, the go-ahead on an initiative, the grant) that a vast disconnect arises, and we forget the natural abilities stories give us.

Show Don't Tell

Stories give you the ability to say something you can't just say. If I tell you, "we are great at customer service", or "community is the center of everything we do", do you believe it? Do you think, "Oh wow, they really care about us, and I feel so connected to this organization"? Yeah no.

As I write this, a popular meme on TikTok is "Tell Me Without Telling Me". As you can guess, the idea is to, for example, tell me you are the middle sibling without telling me you're the middle sibling. One girl described living temporarily outside her family home and coming home to find the house empty. The family had moved away without telling her.

> Stories give you the ability to say something you can't just say.

Same idea. Tell me you are great at customer service without telling me you are great at customer service. Now, that would be a story.

A regional healthcare provider engaged me to help them do a better job of telling their story. They wanted the community to understand that they serve all ages at every stage of their lives – regardless of their ability to pay (self-insured, insured, veteran, uninsured). Specifically, they wanted to bust the common misperception that they were just a meth treatment facility. But you can't come out and say, "We aren't just for meth addicts anymore". So, how do we say it without saying it? We look at the lives they are changing every day for the better, and we tell those stories. We look to kids and vets, from pediatrics to geriatrics, and we tell the stories.

Your stories are a prime opportunity to tell people something that you can't just say about yourself. The next time you find yourself struggling because you don't want to brag about your organization, ask what story will make the point for you.

Make Meaning Out of Data

Recently I tried to decipher a voter's pamphlet received in the mail to prepare for the upcoming election. But I couldn't focus on the content and had to reread it several times to grasp the concepts. I still didn't get it – the language was riddled with legal and political jargon and double negatives that made it impossible to follow, let alone grasp the meaning. I finally resorted to asking a friend who is immersed in local politics. Her values align with mine, so I gave up and asked her who I should vote for.

> If you make your audience work hard to understand, you will lose them and remain ignored.

Now imagine your audience experiencing the same confusion about the work you are putting out to the world. You are completely immersed in your work, and it makes perfect sense to you, but your audience isn't getting it. As to the voter pamphlet, I am a conscientious citizen and had to get to the bottom of the situation. Otherwise, it would have been easy enough to give up and move on. If you make your audience work hard to understand, you will lose them and remain ignored.

Humans are meaning-making machines with extremely short spans of attention. Give us a bunch of dry data and facts, and our brains "default" to figuring out what it all means – if we're so inclined. If it takes too much work and we aren't invested enough, we won't take the time. We move on. There's plenty of competition for our attention.

What if you made it easy for your audience and did the work for them? Your favorite news outlet does this every day. They make sense of what is happening in the world and report it to you. Take a piece of legislation recently passed by Congress as an example. Most people don't have the time or energy to read an Act of Congress; we rely on the media to sort through the details and report what they think we need to know. This opens a separate debate on the role of media

22

and our human tendency toward confirmation bias, but these are conversations for another day!

Think like a news producer and do the work for your audience, so they don't have to. Ask yourself one question (that will lead to a few others) before you recite a bunch of facts and data out to the world. Do the work for them and explain: What does this mean to the people we are trying to reach? Why should they care?

Give Life to Statistics

John Le Carré wrote, "Stats and numbers are abstract. When we take a statistic down to a single number, we breathe life into the point".

This quote is notable because stats and numbers are not really abstract – they are entirely concrete. The problem is, we become numb to numbers. I heard on the news that a global drug ring was busted and 52 tons of cocaine confiscated. Talking about this on our morning run, I asked friends what 52 tons even looks like. It's hard to fathom, isn't it?

A story allows you to breathe life into your statistics. Nicole Grimm's story about the girl working at the pizza place gave life to the huge number of patients the clinic serves annually. When we hear about the people behind these numbers, we think, "Oh wow. I had no idea," just as Nicole didn't realize that she might have bought a pizza from someone struggling in her community.

Don't get me wrong. I do understand it in the abstract (there goes that word again). But when you tell me the story of what actually happened, I totally get it. And I am more likely to take action, which might be as simple as voting for you to win the grant money.

Cut Through the Noise

This is the bonus superpower of stories. They let people get to know you, which is the richest and most beautiful thing you can do. Your stories set you apart from everyone else doing the same or similar things to you. People will either latch onto your stories or not. If they don't, it's because they weren't the right fit. I know that's scary as you want everyone to love you, but telling stories opens you to criticism. It will take some risk and make you a little vulnerable, and maybe you feel you can't afford that.

You can't afford not to.

When I turned thirty, my hair began to turn gray, and I promptly went to the salon to get it colored. I kept up this routine of getting a color every month and flat ironing it straight to look polished and professional for some twenty years. I even did the Brazilian Blowout for many of those years. Then, in 2019, I decided to stop. To be fair, I stopped because I hated spending two hours in the hair chair every month (yes, I could not go longer than four weeks), I hated putting chemicals on my head, and I wanted all that time back.

The transition was emotional, as I had no idea what was hiding underneath that color. I was worried that my very silver hair would age me. Did I look like an old lady now? But here was the unexpected outcome. I had spent decades making myself look like I felt like I should look. That was a lot of work to fit in. Boring.

Now, I have this huge mess of curly silver hair that drives me crazy more often than not, but I get stopped all the time by strangers who tell me they love my hair. I stood on my lawn one day, and a woman riding by on her bike did a double-take and shouted over her shoulder, "I love your hair". I walked by a woman at the airport, who said, "I love your hair". My husband gave me a knowing smile, as he was the one who had encouraged me from the beginning.

After spending so much time trying to fit in, I finally stood out by showing up as me – and people loved it. They were attracted to it.

> "Your story is not a tool to make people believe something that isn't true."

You can do the same by revealing who you are as an organization – from boring to galvanizing to emotionally connected.

"Your story is not a tool to make people believe something that isn't true," Wes King, owner of Tahoe Trail Bar, explained on my Breaking Trail Podcast (Gerber, 2019). He's right; your story is a tool to let people know who you are. It is a tool to help people understand, trust, and want to be involved with you. It enables you to stand out in the crowd and go from So What? to So Funded!

To build those tools, you need to find the story – we'll do this in the next part, Discover.

But before you move on, think deeper about your use of stories:

- What do you want to brag about?
- How can you tell us about it without telling us?
- How can you help your audience make meaning of the facts and data you share?
- Look at the statistics you use to make your case. How can you bring those numbers to life through a story?

You are the hero about to embark upon a journey. As the news producer for your team, you'll start as an investigative reporter. Get your team together, get them on board, and use the previous chapters to help you make a case for those dubious about the mission ahead. Have those necessary and difficult conversations, knowing that everyone will thank you for it later because you are leading them.

By now, you'll have some ideas in place for your story strategy. You'll know what you are trying to achieve and who you are trying to reach. You may have identified the types of stories you want to tell. You may not know yet. That's where Discover will help you listen out for the stories you need to tell.

Ready?

DISCOVER

Welcome to the Discover phase. I call it StoryListening because your curiosity, attention, and ability to listen will be central to the material you gather and the stories you can tell.

This section is foundational to making your storytelling efforts more effective, and it removes the pressure for you alone to develop content. For example, a client sent me a draft messaging plan for an announcement they would soon be making about their rebrand. She said it was just a draft and that she still needed to "bring the love" and add emotion to it.

We reviewed it together. It contained phrases like "our values", and "excited about our rebrand", and "updating our social media profiles". There's nothing wrong with this, but I call it "So what?" content. Someone sat down in front of a blank screen, and this is all they could come up with.

If you have a bank of stories ready to draw from, you have substance, not filler. You have meaning, not generalizations.

Are you ready to embark on your role as the news anchor/producer in your team? In this phase, you'll learn to take all the activities and events around you and your team to curate and package them into stories that will move your audience.

You can determine what information and which people to pursue to gather your stories through the power of inquiry. Then, when you sit down to write that rebranding messaging, you can speak to specifics that relate to the people consuming your stories. When they relate to it, they attach to it.

PLAN

"Times of transition are strenuous, but I love them. They are an opportunity to purge, rethink priorities, and be intentional about new habits. We can make our new normal any way we want."

– Kristin Armstrong, cyclist and three-time Olympic gold medalist

A story plan should look like Google Maps directions when you have weak internet.

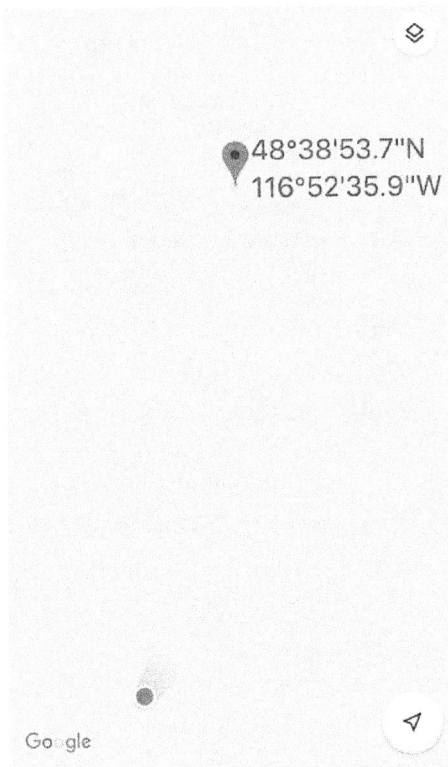

48°38'53.7"N
116°52'35.9"W

Google

You know where you are (sort of), and you know where you want to go. Google shows where you are relative to your destination but doesn't have enough connection to give you the route, so you have to feel your way around. And that's my advice to you for a story plan. Figure out where you are now and where you want to go (this will involve internal reflection within your team). Then, we'll have a process for feeling your way to the destination (this will be your external investigation), where you'll find the people to talk to and uncover the stories you don't know are out there.

The process is simply a matter of the Why, the Who, and the What.

Why? Be clear as a team on why you are doing what you are doing.

Who? Who are you trying to reach?

What? What questions must you ask to get there?

WHY?

Does everyone in the organization know and agree on what success looks like? Maybe your Executive Director doesn't feel you need to focus on fundraising. For her, what matters is shaping community opinion around a particular issue. But the Board wants to see ROI on their storytelling, as they think it's fluff. Yet, we know that when done well, storytelling is highly strategic and makes change happen. You might need to start small and show the value, one story at a time.

Regardless of your position in the organization, it is always helpful to have this conversation to ensure alignment. Is this about a capital campaign? Fundraising targets? Shifting perceptions?

Think about where you landed on the model on page 29. That will help you determine where you are now and where you want to go.

The stories you tell move your audience up the ladder while simultaneously elevating your standing in your community. Understanding where you are at any given time helps you know what kind of stories you need to share.

Typically, the answer to the "Why?" question falls in one of three categories:

1. **Captivate**: Make them aware of something.
2. **Motivate**: Change the way people think.
3. **Activate**: Take action, such as donate, vote, sign, or attend an event.

How Will You Measure It?

Storytelling is hard to measure because the outcomes are often based on intangibles such as awareness and perception. In the Leverage section of the book, you'll find information on measuring outcomes. For now, keep in mind which metrics you can track that are indicators (either real-time or lagging) for your efforts. For example, to track awareness, you might measure audience numbers, such as traffic to specific pages on your website, subscribers to your email list, followers on your social media platforms, or attendees at your physical events. Measure them year on year.

Measure engagement and perception by clicks and opens in your email campaigns, shares, and comments on your social channels. If you host a public event and gather input, track positive and negative sentiment.

Action is easier to track because it typically involves giving, attending, or signing, and these numbers are tangible – how many volunteers showed up, how many dollars were raised, or the number of signatures on a campaign.

Having chatted about this with Johna Burke, the CEO of AMEC (International Association for the Measurement and Evaluation of Communication), I can barely scratch the surface of the topic in this book. For the ultimate resource in learning about measurement and evaluation, go to www.amec.org.

"In the planning piece, make sure your metrics are SMART. They should be specific, measurable, achievable, relevant, and time-bound," said Johna. We'll hear more from her later.

Knowing what you want to track will drive your call to action, so have the metrics in place from the start. To see how engaged people are with your email campaign, provide a link for them to read more.

> Your stories should always have a next step for the audience.

Your stories should always have a next step for the audience; a "Now what?" Continuing to ask how you will measure something gives you the discipline of including that next step. We'll get into this more later. For now, make sure you know if and what you are tracking.

WHO?

Do you know what kills a story? When no one cares about it. To get people invested enough to take action, we have to make them care. And to do that, we need to have a pretty good understanding of who they are, what they care about, and what keeps them up at night. Where are they gathering and meeting? Where are they consuming content?

The best way to get that information is to talk to them. Conduct interviews and put out surveys. Ask donors why they give. Ask benefactors how your organization has helped. Look at community members and get perspectives and opinions on both sides of the issues. If you are in advocacy, why do people feel one way or another? How do they make decisions, and what information will they need from you to do so? Schedule interviews, create a survey, host a community or stakeholder meeting to learn these things.

What questions will you ask? That depends entirely on what you want to know.

Typically, we want to know their understanding of your organization. You could ask them how they would describe you to someone else. What is their experience with you? (Whether a donor, a volunteer, staff, someone you've helped, they all have an experience they can share.)

What do they think would happen if you didn't exist? I like asking this question because it reveals what's at stake. Good stories have big stakes.

If you are conducting a survey or poll, consider giving them the option of sharing their contact info so you can follow up for any story gathering. Your questions should elicit the beginning of the story, giving you enough to decide to want to pursue it further. If you like something you see, follow up and ask for an interview, and this will provide a well of story sources for you.

WHAT?

What stories do you want to tell? To be an effective storyteller, you have to tell an effective story. Once you've learned where you stand with your audience, you have a better idea of your priorities – from awareness to perception, building trust, and influencing action. It's helpful to take it a step further and engage your team on a journey of internal reflection.

In his book *A More Beautiful Question,* Warren Berger shows how organizations make innovative breakthroughs through the power of inquiry (Berger, 2014). Using a different set of questions, I believe we can effect change through investigation. These questions will help you build a list of stories you'll want to pursue.

It might be helpful to start a spreadsheet to capture these ideas. I've included a template at the back of the book, or you can create your own with column headings that include: Topic idea, Author, Person to interview, Quarter (when the story should run), Story type (i.e. understanding, perception, action).

The Four Questions

Question One: Awareness – How do you want to be seen?

Jeff Bezos said, "Your brand is what other people say about you when you're not in the room." Review the data collected from your surveys and interviews. What are people saying about your organization? Does it align with how you want to be seen?

> Remember, stories are more powerful when they show rather than tell something.

What stories can you tell to shift the conversation? Remember, stories are more powerful when they show rather than tell something.

I work with an Education Alliance that exists to support the school district in their community. They want to be a credible, nonpartisan source of information. This drives much of their work as they don't want to be seen as pandering to the school district or promoting a political agenda. For example, when the school levy went to vote, they had to be careful to show why the levy existed (because of the whacky funding formula). Their goal was to inform, relying on the fact that adequately informed public were more likely to vote in favor of the levy without explicitly being asked to do so.

> *For you:* How would you like to be seen? For people to think or see that way, what do they need to know, and who can tell that story?

Question Two: Understanding – Is there a consensus that the problem is real?

There is often a disconnect when people don't understand that you solve real problems. Your organization exists to change something for the better, to fix what isn't working. Does the world agree with you? Do they believe it is a problem worth solving?

One healthcare nonprofit I spoke with is working to achieve equity in healthcare. This is important, but do people truly recognize there is inequity in the American healthcare system? That might seem like a silly question, but be sure and challenge your assumptions. It's easy to become so immersed in the work that you never question whether others are on the same page.

Let's return to the Education Alliance. The public didn't understand why it was necessary to support the school district. They assumed that their tax dollars funded the school district and didn't understand that this wasn't enough. The school budget lacked funding for many programs that brought enormous benefits to the students and the community.

This generated a need for many stories. We realized we needed to show how the funding formula worked; what was and wasn't included. That was helpful, but we also wanted to show how other programs benefited students. For example, we found a high school graduate who attended a conference that the curriculum wouldn't cover (but that my client funded). At this conference, she learned about photojournalism and decided that was the career she wanted to pursue. She is now a creative director at Time Magazine.

The community has a large retired population, so we had to make a case for them to support the school district when they don't have children in the system. We found doctors and retailers who moved to the area – thanks to the quality of schools. If this population wanted basic services in their community, they needed to support the school district, even when their children had long since graduated from it.

> *For you:* Explore the problem you solve at individual, community, and society levels. What stories can you tell to demonstrate that this problem exists? Why should they care?

Question Three: Trust – What are the objections and potential pushbacks?

Hypothetically, your audience is in three groups. One is staunchly opposed, the second includes raving fans and supporters, and the third sits on the fence (for any number of reasons).

In my experience, you won't persuade the detractors to shift their thinking. If we assume they have deeply ingrained values that won't change, it's useless and exhausting to try. But it's important to know what they are saying and why they are opposed to you. This allows you to frame stories against these arguments when addressing the fence-sitters. They'll hear something from your detractor and want to learn more. You build trust by addressing tough topics head-on.

You build trust by addressing tough topics head-on.

Here's a simple example of a grant application for a SmartPalate technology system that helps children with speech impediments. Knowing that the funder uses the cost per person served as criteria for acceptance, the grant application said:

"I respect that this is a very expensive grant application that would affect only a few students. Working in the special services department, I see the staggeringly disparate needs of students. I see how some students require an astounding degree of resources while others need hardly any to achieve a moderate level of success. What this grant is asking for is a gift that many of us take for granted. A gift that most of us need hardly any additional resources to achieve, but that will affect these students' daily interaction, every day of their lives – a clear, confident voice."

I love this example for understanding the question in the funder's mind. In addressing it upfront, the grantee established trust and made a strong argument for the need, despite the extra cost.

I'll come back to that idea in Question Four, but first, let's look at bigger-scale objections that you are sure to encounter. These might be about you as an organization and how you manage funds, or they might be around your cause.

An animal welfare organization I worked with faced reputation issues when a few disgruntled former staff members circulated social media comments attempting to discredit the Executive Director. They claimed that the shelter was largely empty, and the organization was turning away owner surrenders. They didn't understand that animal welfare has evolved, and the goal is now to keep animals out of cages, relying on home-to-home relocation and/or fostering. Pets were turned away due to COVID restrictions.

Better Together prepared a series of scripted responses to highlight the evolution of animal welfare. It began with a brief introduction from the Executive Director explaining their mission to enhance the connection between humans and their pets. She shared the number of animals they had helped over the past year and how they had done so with fewer animals physically in the shelter. Then, an owner shared how relieved they were to have found a new home for their dog without needing to leave them at the shelter.

The shelter told a positive story that proactively countered the arguments – without calling out those arguments. In this way, they told their side of the story without appearing defensive and without raising objections that might not have existed previously.

That last point is important, so I'll repeat it. You don't want to raise objections that did not exist before. Objections from a small minority don't mean everyone is paying attention. Here's a similar case in point. When Tesla CEO Elon Musk was personally insulted by reporter James Broder's negative review in the *New York Times* (Broder, 2013), he responded with a point-by-point rebuttal in his blog (Musk, 2013). Broder promptly came back with a second article shoring up his arguments (Broder, 2013). If someone hadn't seen the first review, they most definitely saw the second because the media picked it up, and it became big news.

> *For you:* As a team, brainstorm all the potential objections and identify the pushback questions people will ask. Decide how to get ahead of these with positively-angled stories that put the argument to rest. Look at what your opposition says to you, in letters to the editor, and on social media. Decide what stories you can tell that prove these statements are untrue or debunk any misperceptions.

I am not suggesting you engage with your detractors directly – although sometimes that might be warranted. Address objections positively, keeping in mind that you want to defuse the situation, not fan any flames.

Question Four: What is this really about? And why should someone care?

You are a complex organization with many stories to tell, each with facets that depend on who you are talking to. Whenever I step in front of an audience to speak or train, I modify the agenda, stories and examples to fit the audience. We're engaging in a conversation. Just like that coffee with a friend, a first date, or a long-time spouse, what you talk about varies.

Spark a conversation by asking yourselves what you are doing and what it is really about. My Education Alliance client funded a grant to bring a fiddle camp to an elementary school. On the surface, that sounds pretty unimportant compared with all the other pressing matters in our world today. Limiting the story to learning how to play the fiddle would likely be unsuccessful. So we asked what this was really about. Well, it changed the culture in the school because everyone was so excited about a break in the academic curriculum. That still gets a "meh". Then, we learned about a shy, reserved girl who got dressed up for her recital and gave an incredible performance despite her nerves. We had a beautiful photo of her on stage and the story, we realized, was about building self-confidence in our youth. It was about pushing their boundaries and helping them step out of their comfort zones.

Take your story a step further and make sure you've tied it into why this really matters. To make it compelling, bring out the facets that get your audience excited.

I don't think there is such a thing as true altruism. People need to know what's in it for them. I'm not a cynic. What's in it for them could be as simple as "it makes them feel good". It's human nature to feel good about contributing to society. But when it comes to funding a school in a remote region on the other side of the world, sometimes it's not enough to simply feel good. We also want to know it's helping our side of the world, especially when there are important causes to consider right here where we are.

> *For you:* What are we really doing here? Elevate the conversation by asking what happens when we are successful at this initiative? Why does this matter? Who is this story for, and what do they care about? Why should they want to help?

YOUR JOURNEY

The answers to these questions should help populate your story spreadsheet. Your next step is to become the assignment desk. Review the ideas these questions create and make an editorial calendar. Don't be daunted by your task; instead, identify the priorities based on how much you can handle. One story per month might be as much as you can do. That means by the end of your first year, you'll have twelve stories from which to draw.

Think about your calendar when working on the timing. Consider organizational and national events and holidays and how you can tie in with those. Think about the timing of fundraising campaigns, your annual gala and your annual report. Adjust the timing to gather stories at the right time rather than scrambling at the last minute to fill your stuff with content. That's when you end up using BS stories because you are sitting at your desk with a blank screen and a deadline.

Record this plan in metaphorical pencil because the story-gathering phase, which we'll talk about next, might change your approach. This process isn't linear, and I encourage you to take each step lightly and with an open mind.

Template:

Start a spreadsheet for your story. Plan:

1. Columns: Topic idea, Author, Person to interview, Quarter (to run), Story type

   _____

   _____

2. Key objectives: make them measurable where possible.

   _____

   _____

3. What are the desired outcomes?

   _____

   _____

4. What are your expectations of the deliverable? Videos, written stories, what else?

   _____

   _____

5. Understand and agree the objectives and metrics from the start.

LISTEN

STORYGATHERER

"Most people do not listen with the intent to understand; they listen with the intent to reply."

– Stephen Covey

Many of us find it easier to develop content on our own. We know this stuff. We've dedicated our lives to it. We understand who benefits from our programs. We know our audience. We know our donors. We figure there's no need to talk with them and get their stories.

Not so fast.

When we operate from a vacuum, we don't realize the assumptions we are making: assumptions about what our audience knows and cares about and what they don't know or care about. We also make assumptions about what we know, which is an even greater danger.

Did you know that frogs have very poor eyesight? In their book, *The Art of Possibility*, Benjamin and Rosamund Zander write that frogs can see light and dark, and that's about it. It gives them the ability to see and catch a fly in the sunlight. They have no idea of the world outside of that (Zander & Zander, 2002). It makes you wonder what we can see and sense and what we have no idea we are missing, doesn't it?

My point is that when you start gathering stories, you learn much about your organization that you never knew. You may even see and think about your organization differently and change the way you talk about it. In doing so, you will resonate more effectively with your existing audience and grow that audience.

I'm guilty of doing what Stephen Covey wisely identified in the quote that opens this chapter. I listen to someone's story, say, about a trip to somewhere I've been, and I am just waiting for a break to talk about my experience. When I do, I'm not really listening to the other person. I'm listening to reply, not to understand. Instead of asking questions to explore, I kill the conversation by turning it back to me. And in doing so, I miss the opportunity for deeper understanding.

Good storytelling starts with good storylistening.

Good storytelling starts with good storylistening. The better the material (research and interviews), the better your story will be.

Once you know the objectives of your story (who you are trying to reach and what message you want to deliver), it's time to find the right people to interview. Introverts will likely push back on this idea. (You thought you could do this storytelling thing from the quiet of your desk and laptop, didn't you?) Those of you pressed for time (who isn't?) are also going to hate me for suggesting it. If you have any other excuses for skipping this section, I urge you not to. I promise it will make your work easier in the long run and vastly improve the quality.

You want to be "pathologically empathic", as Ann Handley explains in her book *Everybody Writes* and to do that requires a level of understanding you can't have when operating purely from the comfort of your own vacuum-based decisions (Handley, 2014).

Dave Gray, the founder of XPLANE and co-author of *Gamestorming*, created the empathy map, a beautiful framework to inspire your questions (Gray, n.d.). If you are visual, you can draw the face of the person and then four quadrants radiating from their head to answer the following questions:

1. What do they see?

2. What do they hear?

3. What are they thinking?

4. What do they feel?

Figure out who you are going to talk to, get introductions where needed, and schedule interviews. Do them in person or video conference – whatever works best for you. I love using Zoom and recording the sessions. I use Otter.ai to provide a transcript, so I can listen to understand rather than take notes.

During the session, I make notes of important points I want to remember. Studies show you are more likely to remember things when you write them down with actual pen and paper. Of course, I also note follow-up questions I want to ask, but I don't usually want to interrupt the person I'm interviewing (unless they go on an unhelpful tangent).

Prepare Your Questions in Advance

I always do my homework before the interviews. If I'm introduced to someone by a third party, I ask why they feel I should talk to them. I do Google searches and check their website where appropriate. After all, I don't want to waste time asking questions if the answers are readily available. The interview is for the stuff you can't Google.

I prepare questions using a basic framework for the three-act story and build from there. Every story has a before, a middle, and an end.

Because you are using this to develop any number of stories from founder/origin, donor, or impact stories (we'll look at these in-depth in Chapter Five), I'm going to be broad here in my descriptions so you can apply them to your specific circumstances.

I prepare all interviewees by explaining the purpose of the story. It should help them frame their responses if they know how and why the story will be used.

1. **Before:** We want to understand the landscape as it stood before anything happened. This is the set-up. What brought the subject to the inciting moment that you'll get to in the next stage of questions. Get a feel for what their world looked like and the problem or conflict they needed to resolve. Remember the empathy map and ask questions that evoke what they were seeing, thinking, feeling and hearing.

    Here are some sample questions:

    *   Describe your situation before you ...

    *   What were the circumstances that led you to...?

    *   How did you feel, or were you concerned? Worried? What were you thinking?

2. **Middle:** This gives us a turning point or transition – a challenge that was met and overcome. To evoke emotion, we need to communicate emotion. Have you ever listened to an interview where the person starts crying, and no matter what they are saying, it makes you cry too? Yep. Emotion is contagious, and if you can't convey it, you won't be able to evoke it in your story.

    > Emotion is contagious, and if you can't convey it, you won't be able to evoke it in your story.

    *   How did the organization or the program change the situation?

- What was the change or the transition like?
- How were others impacted?

3. **After:** This is the outcome and the lessons learned; it's where we communicate the resolution of the problem and share any advice or takeaways for the audience. This provides an opportunity to relate.

    - If you had it to do again, what would you do differently?
    - What was the most significant thing you learned?
    - What would you say to people who are in a similar situation?
    - Now that this has happened, what is possible for you? (This will help you answer Question Four in the planning section, "What is this really about and why should someone care?")

Always end with a question that draws out anything else you'd like to know. "Is there anything you'd like to share that I didn't think to ask?" Often, they feel relaxed when the interview is nearly over and have some great additional thoughts. Your interviewee will need to know the objective of your story to help you with this last bit.

Troubleshooting the Interview

I tend to find myself in trouble now and then and fall back on a few linchpin prompts to help. For example, if I'm worried about asking a question that is too personal or prying, I'll start with "Do you feel comfortable" or "If you feel comfortable, can you tell me…."

If we are in an area I don't quite understand, I might say, "Forgive my ignorance, but can you explain…." If you don't get it, others might not. Don't be afraid to get further explanation.

If an interviewee isn't particularly helpful – perhaps being rather vague or broad, I might get them to dig deeper by asking them for a specific example. "Can you remember a time when this happened?" Or "Can you give me a specific example?"

STORYLISTENER

When you embark on the story discovery phase, resist the urge to let preconceived notions inform your process. Instead, go with an open mind of inquiry and let that drive the process. Let the responses lead you to unexpected places. That's often where the good stuff turns up.

I love skiing a mountain I'm not familiar with. (If you aren't a skier, imagine you're visiting a foreign city for the first time.) I love that sense of discovery when you see an opening in the trees (maybe it's an enticing alley), and off you go to see what is in that direction. The risk is you might dead-end and have to climb back up. Maybe you have to bushwhack your way back to safety. That's the cost of admission, and it's OK. But sometimes, just sometimes, you are rewarded with a secret stash of blissful powder (or a romantic café on a quiet, leafy square). It's hard to beat that feeling of discovery.

Now, imagine you are interviewing someone, and they give you similar openings. I recall when someone said, "I moved to California on a whim..." and moved on quickly to tell a different story. I let him go but made a note and asked him later. Those are the openings in the trees that I like to explore. "Earlier, you mentioned you moved to California on a whim. Tell me more about that." And when he responded with, "Actually, it's a pretty funny story...." As he went on to explain, I realized I had found the gold I needed to tie my story together.

Sure, sometimes I get a boring response or something that doesn't work – then I simply move on. Next question. But when you get good at looking for the openings in the trees, you start finding those secret stashes more often, and your story becomes so much more powerful.

Follow that framework and look for the openings. Dig into greater detail.

INTERVIEWER

Honing your interview skills is always a good idea. Curiosity opens many doors and applies beyond storytelling. I also find it useful in social occasions. People love talking about themselves, and when you ask interesting questions, you build better relationships. Good questioning also comes in handy when I'm on discovery calls with potential clients. They are always impressed when I ask insightful and thought-provoking questions. Here are some ways I've cultivated and continue to cultivate my investigative nature.

I started my own podcast, *Breaking Trail,* which puts me in the interview hot seat every other week. I also listen to podcasts and news segments with a second lens; that of the interviewer. Aside from consuming the content, I'm listening to how the interviewer asks questions. Follow great interviewers you enjoy. I think Howard Stern is an incredible interviewer. I know what you're thinking – you can't stand his show. I listen to him for the interviews! (Yes, I know – like people read Playboy for the articles.) But seriously, listen to him interview Chris Martin from Coldplay as an example. He walked us through his creative process for one of their hits, Viva La Vida, and I listened rapt with attention as Stern asked the questions I was dying to ask. It's as though he read my mind and asked exactly what I hoped to learn (Stern, 2016).

> The better the material you gather, the better your outcome will be.

YOUR JOURNEY

Armed with your plan and your questions, you are now ready to head outside into the real world, to talk to real people like an investigative reporter. Rather like foraging for goods to bring to your family, you are scouring for bits of goodness to bring back to your desk. Enjoy this phase. Embark upon it with a sense of inquiry. Let your curiosity drive the process. Watch for the openings in the trees and go there courageously. If you have to bushwhack your way out, know it's the cost of admission. Don't let it discourage you; instead, keep your eyes out for the next opening.

The better the material you gather, the better your outcome will be. When you follow this process, the stories come through you rather than from you. I find that to be liberating. It also makes the job much easier, and you'll find that becoming a master storyteller might not be as hard as it sounds.

Helpful Tip

Start early and maintain a database of stories, quotes, statistics, and studies as you come across them. Try keeping them in story folders such as donors, clients, or internal. You also might have different programs or categories you want to use. I find Evernote helpful and use the tagging system to quickly find a quote from a donor. This process might feel like overkill initially, but trust me, it will be easier if you start with a good system. You want something searchable, so when you need a particular anecdote or quote, you can readily access it to use in an email campaign, a speech for the executive director, a welcome or thank you letter.

DREAM

"No matter what you do, it somehow goes into the music; you can just tell it's not coming from an honest place."

– Elton John (John, 2019).

Now feels like a good time to talk about the creative process. It's more than likely that you don't consider yourself creative. I'd like to dispel you of this notion right now and help you tap into a creative space to listen to your intuition.

In his autobiography, Me, Elton John referred to Victim of Love, one of his worst performing albums. It was created out of contractual obligation with a label he no longer wanted to work with. "Making an album in bad faith is never a good idea," he said. You can tell when your heart isn't into something (John, 2019).

What you put into your work is what your work will convey.

> What you put into your work is what your work will convey.

Stories are not a trick to get people to support you. They are not a hack. Instead, they channel the excellent work you do into a compelling emotional connection and evoke the question, "what do you need?" from your supporters.

If your heart isn't into it, your audience will sense that.

So, let's honor their time and intelligence, and I'll share my creative process for story development. Take what works for you and modify what doesn't.

There's no template for storytelling – although many will argue this point. If storytelling were a six-step process, we'd all be doing it well, and you wouldn't need this book. But stories would be boring because we'd all be following the same formula. (I'm looking at you, rom-coms – a dying movie genre.) OK, so I'll contradict myself in the next chapter on structure, but my point is precisely that. There are rules, formulas, and processes to creating great stories, and they are all meant to be broken.

Before I start writing or scripting a story, I think about the creative direction for the work. I want a sense of what the story will look like, so I know the plan when I sit at my desk. This prevents procrastination, by the way. If I know where to begin, I don't dread the process. And yes, I know that getting started is the hard part.

I must do several things to get to the point where I have a concept or creative direction in mind. These aren't specific moments but more states of mind that I flow through. They include assessing the materials I've gathered, accessing my creativity, and connecting the dots. It's not a linear process because an idea or direction might have sparked from a comment from your interviewee or a surprising statistic from a survey you completed.

ASSESS

Get Out of Your River of Thinking

Here's the problem. You can't just turn on creativity when you need it. Do you ever wonder why that best idea came to you while you were in the shower, drifting to sleep, or running in the woods?

In his book, *The Organized Mind,* author and neuroscientist Daniel Levitin explained that our brains work in two phases for creative problem-solving. The first phase involves gathering all the facts using our left prefrontal cortex and anterior cingulate (Levitin, 2014). You've done this already in the plan and storylistening chapters of this book.

The plan identifies your objective, target audience and priorities, and the stories you want to pursue. You've gathered your materials, including studies, facts, and data. You have anecdotes from your interviews. Perhaps you have a quote or two worth sharing from the interviews or from a leader in the work you are doing.

Now, through review, you will assess your materials and identify patterns or themes, so you can decide how to put the story together.

There are many ways to do this, so you should adopt what works best for you. I prefer to work with pen and paper at this point, as staring at a screen doesn't inspire me. I might print all the materials and spread them out on my work table, alongside large flip pad paper and Post-it notes.

Mind maps are incredibly helpful, so I'll write my idea statements on Post-its and start sorting them. Categories filter up to the top, then singular words. I'll draw a map or model on the flip pad paper and start moving the Post-it notes around to find a flow or structure. If you are more digitally minded, apps like Airtable or Prezi might work better for you.

If the story in question is short form, such as an essay or a social post, I'll just take a piece of standard paper and start to outline my ideas.

I need to think like a news producer, so I'll be pondering plenty of questions to figure out what this is really about. A story or a statistic says something, but I need to elevate it to a bigger picture. If I can, I'll bring it to one word. Perhaps this is about connection or confidence, or empowerment. I'll look to find any patterns in the material – repetition and contradiction – and consider what they mean.

I'm taking it all in and consuming it all. At this point, I don't worry about drawing conclusions, I'm just bringing it all into my prefrontal cortex and anterior cingulate. (I don't worry about *where* in the brain it goes; I just bring it into my brain.)

Daniel Levitin elaborated on that first phase of creative problem-solving, saying "...focus all (your) attention on the aspects of the problem as it is presented, or as (you) understand it, combing through the different possible solutions and scenarios with (your) left prefrontal cortex and anterior cingulate. But this is merely a preparatory phase, lining up what we know about a problem."

ACCESS

Giving Yourself Time and Space

Once you've gathered the materials into your brain, that brings us to the second phase, in which Levitin offers that we need to relax, let go of the problem and let networks in the right hemisphere take over. Neurons in the right hemisphere are more broadly tuned, with longer branches and more dendritic spines.

Hold on to your hats, friends – this is the shower moment!

As Levitin says, "When the brain is searching for insight, these are the cells most likely to produce it. The second or so preceding insight is accompanied by a burst of gamma waves, which bind together disparate neural networks, effectively binding thoughts that were seemingly unrelated into a coherent new whole. For all this to work, the relaxation phase is crucial."

The former head of innovation and creativity at Disney, Duncan

Wardle, supports this, saying we can't access our right hemisphere when our brain is in "beta busy" – sitting at our desks, responding to email pings, Slack dings, and text dongs. Think about the last argument you had, where the killer one-liner came to you after you walked away. But not during the fight, right, because you were in beta busy. Being in your cubicle equates to being in your argument (Wardle, 2016).

That is why I can justify getting up from my desk and going for a trail run to work through a problem. It's written in my bio that I might be out in the woods and unavailable to take your call because I'm out doing my best work. This ritual helps me access my creativity. I don't share it for you to replicate, but to inspire you to create one that works for you.

Change the Story You Tell Yourself

Hack your mindset. When Olympic medalist Dan Collins first launched his management consulting practice, his self-limiting beliefs often got in the way of his success. He'd be in the cab on the way to a pitch, and his thoughts might tell him that he wasn't good enough. Other days, that voice would pump him up and say that he was going to nail it. Either way, those thoughts didn't serve him. So, he reminded himself to stay focused on the facts and the task at hand and to disregard, and even disbelieve, his thoughts. He would tell himself, "I am unbelievable". (Collins, 2021)

So, if you are telling yourself you are not a writer or not creative, instead, say you are unbelievable and get on with the project at hand.

Create a Sanctuary

Elton John has recorded albums the world over and said the place where he records has a distinct influence on the outcome of the work. On working in California: "rather than making an album in London when it's pissing with rain every day, it's as if the warmth gets into your bones and relaxes you, and the sunlight somehow glows in the music you make".

We all do our best creative work at certain times of the day and in particular work environments.

For me, the morning hours just after an early trail run in the woods are ideal. Therefore I schedule the work so I know exactly when it needs to happen. Writing this book in hour increments is another. I am fresh off a sweaty workout, showered, dressed for a day at work, and a hundred percent immersed. One hour.

What works best for you?

Next is the working environment. I don't care if it's the kitchen table or a corner of the bedroom, but I like to do something that symbolizes that creative work is happening. It might be as simple as my favorite mug of coffee or a candle to create ambience. We aren't Hemingway, after all. I'm not suggesting you build a tiny house in the woods (although Ann Handley and many others have done so), but I think it's awesome if you can.

Invite the Muse

Stick with me here, as I'm not joking – but I'm also not going to get all metaphysical on you. (Well, maybe a tiny bit.) In all my reading and listening about the creative processes of great storytellers and artists, I have seen a pattern. (Yes, I'm about to talk about patterns in the next section so take note.)

The pattern is that creative genius comes through you, not from you.

If you want to know more, listen to Elizabeth Gilbert's Ted Talk *Your*

Elusive Creative Genius (Gilbert, 2009) or read Steven Pressfield's book, *The War of Art* (Pressfield, 2002). Pressfield explains genius as "a Latin word; the Romans used... to denote an inner spirit, holy and inviolable, which watches over us, guiding us to our calling".

> Creative genius comes through you, not from you.

See? This takes some of the pressure off you, doesn't it? And if you do as Pressfield does, you can invoke the muses. His way is by reading the invocation in the opening to Homer's *Odyssey*. I recommend a Google search or reading his book to check it out for yourself.

I let ideas bounce around in my head and marinate until I determine a starting point or creative direction. Then I know what to do when I'm in front of the computer. It's the best prevention for procrastination.

CONNECT

In the Distill section of this book, I'll dedicate plenty of time to simplifying the key points of your message. Clarity is at the core of this work. In the Discover phase, however, I encourage expansive thinking. From gathering your stories to assessing your materials and accessing your creativity, you should be exploring, curious, on a journey. You will be accepting dead-ends with inevitability. Ideas are to be explored, not eliminated. Yet.

Approach this phase like a joyful puppy.

In 2015, we adopted a six-month-old Bernese Mountain dog and our first several months with him (as any puppy parents will understand) were certainly a trial. Don't get me wrong: he was (and is) sweet and precious and a bundle of joy, but my first observation as a new puppy mom is that plenty of crushing of unbridled enthusiasm takes place;

much boundary setting and the use of restraining words such as "stay" and "no" in response to their sheer wonder at the world.

Discover is the joyful puppy phase, with unbridled curiosity and enthusiasm.

Bringing It Together: The Shower Moment in the Checkout Line

In 2019, I was engaged by an animal welfare organization to help them rebrand and rename. I can admit this now, but I am not a naming expert. I say that because I didn't think I had the creativity, but more importantly, I had never named things, at least not organizations, before.

I took on the project because the Executive Director was (is) smart and led the way in animal welfare evolution. I wanted to be a part of that. I also love dogs and animals, even though I crush puppy souls. She explained that their mission is to enhance the lives of pets and their humans, and how one goes about that mission can vary. The "evolution" in animal welfare is that animals in cages do not enhance anyone's lives, and it is possible to help communities without putting pets in the shelter. (Their programs support this effort too.)

I agreed that their name, Panhandle Animal Shelter, no longer told the story of their mission – they were so much more than a shelter. And because they served an area larger than the panhandle of Idaho, the geographic "tag" on their name didn't serve either. Their story had evolved, and they needed a new title. So, here's what we did.

We scheduled a stakeholder workshop to ask the internal questions you read in the Plan chapter. Then we conducted a community survey so that we could review the responses during the meeting. The surveys included many of the questions detailed in the storylistening phase. From those responses, we chose a small handful of stories to pursue. People had given us their contact information if they were willing to share more and be interviewed.

I had Post-it notes stuck to butcher paper, meeting notes, and data from the Executive Director. They provided me with studies on the benefits of pet ownership. Then I asked for several weeks to come back with a possible name and preliminary messaging. I was terrified. What if I couldn't think of anything?

As glamorous as it may sound, creativity under pressure is not fun.

I procrastinated for a week. Three to four weeks felt like plenty of time, so I figured I'd get to it soon.

Then, I made myself sit down and review everything. I processed the notes into an organized document with categories and highlighted things of interest. I asked myself the big question. What is this really about? My answer: It's about the symbiotic relationship between pets and their people. It was a pattern that kept showing up. The studies show the mental health benefits of having a pet. The line about rescue dogs, "who rescued who?" is so accurate. One of the survey questions asked people what our community would be like if the organization didn't exist. (That's the "what's at stake" question) and many people said they couldn't even imagine that situation.

With all this information fresh in my brain, I entered phase two of the creative process. I let it sit and marinate and bounce around in my brain. Quite literally, I slept on it. I paid attention to things around me, to ideas and thoughts as they surfaced, and started a list. No matter how stupid they seemed, I wrote them down.

That weekend, on a trip out of town, I stood at the checkout line in the grocery store waiting for my turn and stared vacantly at

People Magazine. On the cover was a photo of a couple – I don't even remember who they were because the headline blinded me to everything else. It said: Better Together. Remember that spark Levitin describes when the neurons in the right hemisphere make connections? It's like an aha moment. At that instant, I knew the new name for the Panhandle Animal Shelter. I presented it to the team, it was approved within months and launched in the next year. Better Together Animal Alliance: because when it comes to humans and their pets, we are all better together.

YOUR JOURNEY

So, you think you aren't creative? It's a story you are telling yourself – and it's pure fiction.

You are now the creative director of your project. Don't underestimate the power of heading out to the woods for a walk or a trail run, or whatever helps you find quiet space. Do the work in the Discover phase because the material you gather is critical to helping your brain find the patterns and make the connections. Give yourself time and space to allow that to happen.

We all have the capacity to be creative.

DISTILL

You've planned, listened, gathered, and reflected. It's time to craft the story because being a good listener is only the start. It's time to take this message and give it some backbone. Your ability to be disciplined is key to crafting a compelling story. You'll need the discipline to give your message structure, and that will require decisions to leave material out – always a hard thing to do.

It will require discipline to show up even when you don't feel inspired. We'll talk about that, so stay with me.

And it will require discipline to level up – to look at your work with a critical eye and solve problems instead of casting insults (at yourself).

I mention the insults because this is typically the part where I can be pretty hard on myself. Giving voice to the story I want to tell takes time. Sometimes genius just flows, but sometimes it's hard. You'll look at a draft and think it's awful, and maybe, like me, you'll equate yourself with the work and think you're terrible at what you do. This is not a helpful belief. The Level Up section will help you through this.

When you've refined your story and transformed something you might have been ashamed of into something you can be proud of, the feeling is that of Type Two Fun. That's the kind of adventure that sucks until you're done. It's when you look back at the mountain you climbed or the big thing you've achieved, and think, "Wow, that was amazing" – having totally forgotten how un-amazing it was in the process. But we keep going because we want that feeling of accomplishment, of having done something worthy.

We're going to start with some helpful tricks on structure. Here we go.

STRUCTURE

"When the bones are good, the rest don't matter."

– Maren Morris, The Bones

Newsrooms around the world create stories out of world events. They decide which stories are interesting enough to run and find a "hook" rather than reciting a list of facts. Your regular Joe Citizen could sit down and read an entire legislative bill (which we all know won't happen), or he could turn on the news to get their take on it. We trust our news channel to sift through the details and pull out what matters so we can make sense of it all, understand how it affects us or the world, and know what to do about it.

We've focused on the "good" part of a good story up to this point. To tell the right, or most effective, story, you've gone through a process of internal inquiry, followed by an external inquiry. You are clear on the messages that will generate awareness, build trust and understanding, make you memorable and eventually influence action. But now you have to craft them.

Elements and structure will give shape to your message. The elements ensure that you are crafting a story and not a narrative or chronology of events. A structural statement will provide you with the discipline to stay on message to achieve the objective of your story.

> Elements and structure will give shape to your message

I find it helpful to start here, either in my head or at the top of my blank screen.

HOOK

A hook is the part of your story that captures attention and interest. It gives your audience the "so what?" Here are a few hacks I use to ensure the story has that hook.

The first comes from the creators of South Park, but I learned about it from Randy Olson in his book, *Houston, We Have a Narrative* (Olson, 2015). Randy is a former scientist turned film director, and he helps scientists use stories so people can understand them. Sounds familiar, doesn't it?

This hack works particularly well for a social media story, a video script or if you are starting a longer article and need to create order from chaos.

Randy introduces the ABT structure used by the creators of South Park for each of their episodes. It looks like this.

A= And

B = But

T= Therefore

This happened **AND** this happened, **BUT** this is the problem, **THEREFORE**, this is what's next or the conclusion.

The ABT template is a great way to take the protagonist and their conflict and make sure you have an interesting story to tell, not just a rambling sequence of events.

If you have a story that is simply, "This happened, and then this, and then this, and then this", it's a chronology of events, not a story. It's something with no consequences, and no addiction value, as in, there's no reason to stick around because we aren't anticipating anything. If you are wondering why your stuff isn't getting any attention, this could be the reason.

The BUT and THEREFORE add the intrigue.

Here is the ABT for this book. We (purpose-driven leaders) want to make the world a better place, AND to do that, we want people on board with the change we hope to make. BUT we don't know how to articulate the issue in a way that gets people to care about it enough to do something. THEREFORE, if we are better at storytelling, we can use it as a catalyst for change.

Can you see how that might help with a creative brief for your next video? Or the caption to a photo you share on Instagram? It's meant to be a handy tool to move the idea of your story forward.

This is a Story about X

Here is one more example of a structure from the producers of radio shows like *This American Life*. Jessica Abel interviewed Alex Blumberg for the book *Out on the Wire*, to learn how they make decisions on the stories they feature (Abel & Glass, 2015). The formula they use is seemingly straightforward, but it's not easy.

This is a story about X (maybe it's a story about cancer)

It is interesting because Y (what is Y – the woman is an oncologist? The man has been a smoker all his life?)

If Y is interesting and unexpected, go. (The oncologist bit could be interesting because she's dedicated her life to fighting cancer, and now she has it. On the other hand, the smoker might be less interesting, because we know smoking causes cancer.)

If Y is not interesting, the story doesn't move forward. (Or, you'd have to find a more compelling angle with the smoker.)

Regardless of how you do it, look for something interesting or unexpected to capture your readers' attention. You'll also want to make sure your hook includes the essential story elements.

ELEMENTS

Taking inspiration from our favorite storytellers in films and books, let's dissect the essential elements of a story. It starts simply enough: You have a protagonist, who goes through some kind of change through a challenge or problem (the conflict), and you have the resolution of that conflict.

As basic as that sounds, I want to take some time to explore each of those elements to make sure you get them right. As Maren Morris sang in her song, *Bones*, "When the bones are good, the rest don't matter."

Protagonist

Every good story has a hero. The mistake many organizations make is to be the hero of their own story. When you do that, you end up talking about yourself and all the wonderful things you've done, the awards you've won, how long you've been in existence. That may be important stuff, but it's not what good stories are made of.

I've got news for you: People don't care about you. They care about how you are changing the world, and more importantly, how they can be a part of that. Eventually, they will care about the other stuff. That might sound contradictory, especially if the story you happen to be working on right now is about your organization. As far as your story goes, your true protagonist is almost always someone other than you. It is your donor, a client, a staff member, or a board member.

Conflict

Every good story has a conflict, which is convenient because every organization exists to solve a problem or fill a gap in society. The mistake we sometimes make is being so focused on what we want our stories to achieve (to generate donations or get volunteers) that we end up talking about things that don't matter to our audience.

Make sure the problem in your story is one your audience cares about, not the one you care about. You might care that you are short of your fundraising target or that your revenue is down this year from last year. But it's not a conflict that will motivate your audience. It might work for NPR and their pledge drive (but does it?), but don't count on it working for you.

Speak to the conflict your audience wants to help resolve.

> Speak to the conflict your audience wants to help resolve.

Resolution

When it comes to the resolution, I like to think of storytelling in nonprofits as having happy endings. We know this isn't real, and I'm certainly not advocating being misleading. A story that inspires people to action provides hope and possibility. If it is hopeless, your readers might throw their arms up and decide there's no point in trying to help.

I like to start any story with a happy ending in mind. I also like to think there are no mysteries in nonprofit storytelling, so I begin with that happy ending. Think about it. Your audience is strapped for time, and we are competing for their attention. We might only have a split second, so why make them work for it?

What does the world look like when you have fully achieved your mission? Don't take this literally. I know you will always have something to focus on. I get that this is idealistic, but bear with me.

> *For you:*
>
> Develop a hook, so you know you have an interesting angle. Use the ABT or the X and Y exercises if they are useful.
>
> Be clear on the key elements in your story.

Next, let's take a look at those elements in different types of stories.

TYPES

"(Start with) something that is real. The emotional connect is the journey the character takes and the battle. Get people to care, and you can make an impact." – Bryan Fogel (Recode Media, 2021).

Remember this one thing, please. We tell different stories to achieve different objectives. Our job is to match the story to the needs of your audience. That is a fancy way of saying "engage in conversation".

Think of storytelling as a courtship with your audience. Your stories reveal the layers of who you are, one story at a time. But I beg you to resist the urge to put too many messages in one story. (I see you out there, wanting to tell them about your award! And your recent certification! And what about the new website? Surely you have to mention that!)

No single story will accomplish all your needs.

No single story will accomplish all your needs.

Just as you wouldn't tell all your stories and secrets on your first date, and you likely wouldn't propose marriage on a first date, no single story you tell will accomplish everything you want it to.

I first started dating Patrick when I'd just moved from Seattle to Idaho for the Marketing Director position at the ski resort. It was two weeks out from the opening day of the ski season, and I had a perfect storm of anxiety swirling in my head. It was a crazy time sorting out who to talk to and how to get things done in a new community, with a new job. Patrick and I had been hanging out a bit, and he had invited me over to his house for dinner.

On the drive over, I did my best to push all my angst about work into a compartment so I could enjoy company with someone in my new town. I opened the door to the smell of someone cooking for me. And there he was, at the stove, working the pan like a chef. He had a fire in the fireplace and a plate of bruschetta on the kitchen bar. You know that feeling when someone shows you kindness when you're trying to be tough?

Yep – I sprung a waterworks leak and fell to the floor in front of the fire sobbing, letting all that stress out, pretty much involuntarily. All that crazy flowing out all over the floor. Patrick placed his hand on my back and let me cry (which, if I'm honest, was the best thing he could have done, but only encouraged me to carry on). You can probably see why we are now married, but I bring this up to make a point. Had that been our first date, I'm pretty sure he would have run for the door. (I'm really surprised he didn't, as it was early on.)

Anyway, don't let all the crazy out on your first date. Instead, put your audience on a need to know basis. Treat stories as layers, revealing what matters at the right point and time, matching the story to the need.

None of this is to say that we are untruthful or misleading. Our stories are *not* a tool to get people to think something about us that isn't accurate. They are a tool to create understanding, build trust, and inspire action.

If you've completed the Discover phase, you have a list of story ideas to pursue and people who can tell those stories. On the other hand, you might still be looking for inspiration for ideas of stories to tell. Regardless of where you are, it's helpful to understand the different types of stories because new ideas might percolate. It's also a secondary way to ensure your communications meet the needs of everyone in your audience. This is represented on the journey model on page 29 from awareness to emotional connection. There is a time and place for each of these stories to be told.

Let's go back to my client in the education sector for examples of what each of these stories would look like. Our objective wasn't necessarily to raise money (although that certainly would be great in the process); it was to raise awareness around how Idaho schools are funded. We wanted to show why it's important for the community to fill in some of the funding gaps.

We also wanted them to vote "Yes" to supplemental school levies (on property taxes) that were on the ballot every two years. There are two things to note regarding the levy. First, there was a great deal of misinformation circulating that opposed them, and second, the area population included a high percentage of retired people. Without children in the school district, they might think voting for a tax levy to support schools was not in their best interest. We had a lot of work to do and many stories to tell.

Positive Appeal: The Impact Story

Inspire to Action

> *"Show your donors the impact of their generosity."*
>
> – Scott Harrison (Harrison, 2018).

I am often asked if it's wiser to share happy stories that inspire or negative stories that can feel more urgent. Studies vary on whether negative or positive messages achieve better results. In my experience, one is not better than the other, and it really depends on your circumstances and organizational needs. We'll talk about both sides of the coin here – the more positive story focused on impact and the negative appeal focused on need. Each has its place.

The impact story creates hope and optimism and shows that donors' money (or time) will be put to good use doing more of what you started. You can prove success.

To garner both moral and financial support, the Education Alliance wanted to show the strength of our school district. No one wants to throw money at a sinking ship. They needed to know how beneficial it was to have a strong school district and its importance for the communities in which they reside.

We tracked down students who had graduated ten years earlier and talked to them about how a grant the Education Alliance had provided directly impacted their success. We spoke to a skilled tradesman who had gone on to a highly paid position with a local manufacturer thanks to welding equipment my client had provided to the school. In addition, we found a high school graduate who had pursued a career in professional cooking after a grant my client funded sent her to see a professional kitchen for the first time.

These impact stories showed business leaders, retirees and parents who might be attracting people to the area how strong the school district was. And it inspired people to do more.

The impact story is helpful if your priority is to be memorable and inspire action. It offers proof to donors and cites a track record of success for those considering giving because, of course, there is always more work to be done, and that is where the need story plays a role.

You might use your impact stories on the homepage of your website, annual reports, donor thank you letters, grant evaluations and social media.

Urgent Appeal: The Need Story

Sometimes you don't have any "solved problems" to talk about, especially if you are brand new or applying for a grant. You might have other impact stories that prove your track record and ability to get things done, but there will be occasions when you'll have to talk about a need that has not yet been solved.

When the COVID-19 pandemic hit, the Education Alliance had to work quickly with the school district to reallocate funds as remote learning meant many grants could not be implemented. Funds were shifted to high-need areas such as social and emotional needs and teacher learning communities to help them transition to remote teaching.

We talked with students who were stuck at home learning and missing out on sports and socializing with their friends. Remote learning had its challenges. We spoke with their parents to see how the kids were adjusting. We did video interviews with teachers who shared their concern for students who hadn't had internet access and hadn't picked up their packets. Teachers described what it was like to suddenly become "YouTubers". Some of them were so dedicated that they shed tears on camera, worried about the kids they were unable to contact.

In Chapter One (Plan), one of the key questions was, "Do we have a consensus that the problem we solve is a problem?" It's tough to make people care if they don't know there is a problem to begin with.

The Need story works best to generate awareness and understanding in those who don't recognize you have a problem to solve. Consider how you want to message this and ensure it aligns with how you want to be perceived. Some organizations will frame it optimistically while others will make it more urgent, often appealing to guilt to move the needle. It all depends on what works for you. You'll want to have that conversation within your organization.

You might use Need stories in grant applications, fundraising appeals, cases for support and on secondary pages on your website as well as social media.

Shift Perception: The Expert Story

Speaking to clients and donors is great, but a third-party expert can give your message gravitas if the situation warrants it. In the age of fake news and increased skepticism, an outside expert who can explain or bolster the problem you solve will go a long way to building trust and credibility.

We were fortunate with our education client to have access to state Senators and school superintendents. Our state Senator explained the funding formula in-depth and answered the question on many people's minds: "How did we get here?" He also shared what was discussed on the legislative floor.

To help gather public input for a brownfield cleanup project that would create an extension to a natural waterfront park, we took a tour with a brownfields analyst from the Idaho Department of Environmental Quality. We recorded video while he walked us through the contaminated property in question. He pointed out remnants of an old smelter that people thought was a natural rock feature but was actually toxic. We asked layman's questions to understand why what looked like a regular piece of land was far from that. We learned how contaminated the soil is and what normal levels should be.

Subject matter experts are most effective at helping shift perception about misunderstandings around the work you do. This is the evidence that will bolster your claims. Subject matter expert content is handy to have so you can add quotes and data to all your stories. Consider putting the entire interview, be it on video, audio or text, on your website's blog or resources page. Any time you cite the content, asterisk or footnote it with a link to the full article on your website. This will give a huge boost to your credibility.

Answer to a Problem: The Organizational Story

Visit www.charitywater.org and you'll find their organizational story loud and clear (Charity: water, 2021).

Let's examine the key elements here:

- "We believe in a world where everyone has access to clean water. Join us." (Happy Ending and a call to adventure. You are the protagonist.)

- "785 million people lack basic access to clean and safe drinking water. We're on a mission to change that." (The conflict)

- "We believe that sustainable work is locally-led. Along with implementing community-owned water projects, our local partners help facilitate comprehensive water, sanitation, and hygiene (WASH) programming to protect everyone's long-term health." (How to resolve the conflict)

Your website's home page serves many purposes and is where we tend to cram every layer of our story. Consider your audience first – they will be a mix of new and returning visitors. Returning visitors should be able to quickly access the information they need to donate or get involved. The primary messaging on the homepage lets people know your story at a glance. It is the finish line moment I shared at the beginning of this book. Your audience has plenty of things competing for their attention, and you only have a split second to cut through it with a sentence or two. What will you do with that time? Tell them about your awards, nonprofit status, and the year you were established?

Or could you tell a story about the conflict, invite them to be part of your story, and explain how together you will give this story a happy ending like Charity: water does? Notice, they also answered questions you have answered in the planning chapter. Why is the problem a problem? Because it affects everyone's long-term health.

Galvanize: The High Stakes Story

Every good story has something at stake. What is yours?

What would your world look like when you have fully achieved your mission, and there is no longer a reason for your organization to exist? Describe it in stunning detail. Use stories as metaphors for statistics.

Every good story has something at stake. What is yours?

In *Erosion: Essays of Undoing*, Terry Tempest Williams painted a picture of our national parks in 2055. The essay entitled The Park of the Future takes visitors to Canyonlands National Park. She describes how access is limited to the park to two "enclosed viewing stations...that are cooled by solar power". The road is now abandoned, "historical scars reminiscent of a time when the world was fueled by gasoline and people drove cars without thinking." Virtual goggles are provided at the lookout stations where visitors can look out at the now barren landscape and see what it looked like decades ago when there were sage, other greenery, trees, wildlife and water in the river. (Williams, 2019).

This image haunts me. Williams brought the issue of climate change to life by showing us what is at stake. The problem is vast and daunting. While most of us know and care about it, and we do our part by drinking water from Hydroflask water bottles and shopping with reusable bags, we know that's not enough.

In this story, Williams showed what will happen if we don't take action today. By choosing one park and one scenario, she changed how I think about a global issue. She holds real estate in my memory, which is a huge feat since I can't seem to remember anything without writing it down. But I can't shake this story from my mind.

Your story could show your audience a future that doesn't include you and them together. Give them impact, make them think, make you hard to shake from their minds.

And then they'll take action.

Provide a Vision: The Origin Story

Your organization's "about" or "origin" story is sometimes referred to as your boilerplate. I can't think of a more boring term for what is so often a very dull paragraph about you. Your origin story is a wonderful opportunity to pull people in to get to know and understand you at a deeper level.

The origin story helps activate an audience that has heard about the work you do. They already understand the problem and the need. Now they are deciding to get involved, but before they do, they often want to know more about you as an organization.

Usually, there is an incident or pivotal moment that brought your organization to life. There are likely highly personal reasons why people are in your leadership, staff and board positions. By the time your audience wants to know these things, they are deciding to do something. This is the vetting stage.

Many get this wrong by sharing the history or timeline of the organization. There might be a time and place for that (on a website page or a grant application), but it's not a story.

A good origin story involves someone (usually a founder) and their personal experience with your cause.

What is the vision for your organization? I don't mean "what is your vision statement?" – I mean, what does the world look like when you achieve your mission? And yes, I get that some missions are ongoing. This is an imaginary world I am asking you to describe, one where cancer doesn't exist; we live in peace; all people have equal rights and access to work and pay and healthcare. Your origin story allows you to show a problem that existed – something your founder was frustrated about, the turning point in that story and what you are working toward.

You'd typically find the origin story on the website's About page, in speeches and public events, cases for support and donor appeals.

Grant applications might include an abbreviated version to fit word counts. Stories in the media are often about you, and many origin stories have been published as books. Some great examples include *Thirst,* by Scott Harrison, founder of Charity: water (Harrison, 2018), *Three Cups of Tea,* by Greg Mortensen, founder of Central Asia Institute (Mortenson, 2006), and *Hands Across the Water,* by Peter Baines (Baines, 2011).

Social Proof: The Donor Story

It's time for dinner, and you're in an unfamiliar city, walking down a street bordered by cafés on both sides. There is an inviting restaurant with every table full, lively chatter and live music playing, but the wait time is twenty minutes. Next door is another restaurant with many tables available. They can seat you now.

Which one do you choose? Assuming you're into having a wonderful experience and good food, and the decision is not about immediate gratification, of course, you'll choose the first. All those people must know something; otherwise, they'd be at the other place too.

Those happy diners are social proof that this restaurant is the place to be. When your donors are willing to share their story, they are all the other people at your tables, letting prospective donors, who are walking by looking in, know they are not alone. They are in good company. And their stories tell them why.

Rachel Beckwith donated her ninth birthday to a charity: water campaign, and fell short of her $300 fundraising goal. She told her mom she'd try again for her tenth birthday. Sadly, she was in a serious car accident and unlikely to make it to her tenth birthday. At the request of a family friend, founder Scott Harrison reopened her campaign to give the family some encouragement. On Rachel's campaign page, Scott found this, written by Rachel:

"I found out that millions of people don't live to see their fifth birthday. And why? Because they didn't have access to clean, safe water, so I'm celebrating my birthday like never before. I'm asking everyone I know to donate to my campaign instead of gifts for my birthday."

Rachel's renewed campaign ended up raising $1,265,823. She died a few days after that car accident, but Scott pledged to honor her legacy. Rachel's mom came to New York City to share the story on morning shows, and he invited her to Ethiopia to see first-hand the impact of her daughter's legacy – to see Rachel's wells.

Your donor database could be a wealth of stories you don't know about. From the smallest to the largest donations, it doesn't matter. What does matter is the intent behind the people who support you every $10 step of the way.

Donors aren't always willing to share their stories. Some may want to remain anonymous, while others feel uncomfortable putting themselves out there. We always respect their wishes and never pressure anyone into something they don't want to do.

I share these story types with you as a reminder that your stories should take your audience on a journey. Incorporating various story types into your plan will give you more depth and breadth. Use the list above and their suggested uses as loosely as possible. Some of your stories

> Your stories should take your audience on a journey

will do everything, from generating awareness to inspiring action. I only wanted to provide a framework to inspire – not a framework to make you perspire. Don't toil away, making sure each of your stories fits in these tidy boxes. Consider the audience journey. Are you pulling them in with a story about the need? Do they see the impact of your work and that the problem to be solved is doable? Do they know enough about you to feel comfortable joining in your quest with money or their time?

YOUR JOURNEY

The Writer. This is a role you didn't foresee taking on when you got into the work. Don't let the job title scare you. You have content from the people you've spoken to based on a solid strategy you've implemented, and tools from this chapter ensure you tell a story that moves your audience through the layers of who you are as an organization. Carry on with courage, but should you find distractions are holding you back, it's time to combat the procrastination and Show Up.

SHOW UP

CRAFT

*"...miraculous turns of fate can happen
to those who persist in showing up."*

– Elizabeth Gilbert (Gilbert, 2015).

You click "new document" and stare at the blank screen. Then, it occurs to you that now might be a great time to purge the junk mail out of your inbox. Maybe you should do a quick search for that replacement lampshade you've been meaning to order. Or send a quick email reply to your colleague regarding that thing she asked you about. Procrastination is evil, is it not?

If this is you, there are many resources out there to inspire you to show up and create. In this chapter, I've curated the ideas that work for me and that I think might work for you in some fashion.

If you've done the work outlined so far, the blank screen is far less intimidating. You have a plan with an objective for the story, and you've gathered the materials and done the interviews. You've stopped doubting your ability to be creative. You even have a structure, so you know what the story is going to be about.

Yet, you still dread the blank screen.

This is a danger zone because if you aren't vigilant, you can fall back into old habits and fill the screen with "So what?" stuff – jargon, corporate and generic terms, and words that don't mean anything.

You've worked hard to get to this point, so approach your time and your working environment as a treat. I make a cup of coffee. I have beautiful flowers in a vase. My desk is clear of everything I don't need at this moment. I've psyched myself by mentally preparing all morning, so when I sit down, I have an idea of where to start.

Dip into the following ideas as needed, and draw upon whatever works for you. Modify the ideas to work in your way. It's impossible to codify a storytelling process.

From Blank Screen to SFD

Imagine you are at the top of a ski run. Maybe it's a double black diamond expert only run. When you stand at the top, it looks really intimidating and steep. Possibly, the tips of your skis are hanging off the edge as you stare down the slope. You stand there with trepidation, wondering if it's safe to proceed and worried that you'll screw up. You muster up the nerve and take your first turn. Maybe you jump in with gusto, or maybe you sidestep in timidly. And then you take another turn. And another. Then you are in it. And it doesn't feel so steep anymore. You look back and see how much you've done, and now you feel liberated. You think, "Oh, I'm doing this. I can keep going." And you let it go.

Welcome to your Shitty First Draft (SFD). Ann Lamott coined the term in her excellent book on writing, *Bird by Bird* (Lamott, 1997). Making the goal an SFD rather than a finished piece of work removes the pressure. Your bar is very low, but who cares because you are writing! And no one is going to read it.

Start with a stream of thought and no ego. You'll be surprised what the simple process of typing your thoughts onto the screen will start to unravel from your creative little brain.

Editing is your friend.

Editing is your friend, but you're not editing yet. You're pouring your heart onto the page.

Talk to Your Imaginary Friend

At this point, I am not thinking about the science or elements of a story. I'm not thinking about being memorable or creating trust, and I'm certainly not thinking about making an emotional connection. Stories do this naturally.

I'm imagining having coffee with a friend and telling her a story. How would I speak to her? I use conversational words. I describe things that need to be described. I give context or background where it's needed. Then, I tell her why she should care.

Start with Heart

I don't judge a book by its cover; I judge it by the first sentence. The beginning of your story is make-or-break time – it's the money moment. Will you do enough for the audience to want to learn what happens?

> The beginning of your story is make-or-break time.

Sometimes I know exactly how the story will start. During the interview process, someone might have said something powerful or an inciting event gives context to the point. Sometimes it's not apparent, and I work on the rest then return to the beginning. That first paragraph deserves the most time and energy, so return to it later if that's useful. Do whatever works.

You might start with a quote – either from someone you've spoken to or someone known in your space. If you do the latter, that's great: just make sure it's someone who aligns with who you are. In other words, don't always resort to the old white guy who said something pithy a few centuries ago.

You could start with an anecdote, or maybe you have a really surprising statistic.

How will you grab us by the lapels and hold us to the wall to get our attention?

Set the Stage

Introduce us to the protagonist, with some basics about who they are and what keeps them up at night. This is information gathered during your storylistening.

Gabrielle Dolan teaches corporate storytelling and suggests you start with the setting. Where and when? (Dolan, n.d.). The answers to these questions could be general or specific. The person could be in the middle of a field or on Michigan Avenue in Chicago. It could be "decades ago" or September 19, 1964. Help orient your audience in time and space at the outset. It gives them context to understand what you are about to share with them.

Make it Relatable

If you want your "friend" to care, it has to be relatable. Somehow, we have to see ourselves in the story or be affected by its outcome – even if it is to feel good about doing something right. I don't believe in pure altruism; if nothing else, people do good because it makes them feel good.

As I'm writing this, Scott Simon has just told a story on NPR about human rights violations in Chinese manufacturing facilities. It's horrible. But if that were the end of the story, I'd move on and forget about it. In terms of a story rating, that sentence gets a "So what?"

Instead, here is how Scott Simon opened the story:

"Look around you as you listen this morning. Chances are good, in fact, overwhelming, that something you can touch right now, your shirt, socks, running shoes, your coffee cup, pen, were made by enslaved and abused workers in China. We have bought products to use every day and every hour without thinking of the true human cost of things that are so cheap" (Simon, 2021).

Scott took something seemingly far removed from my world and brought it within my fingertips. His story explained the human cost of producing cheap goods and then shared what I could do about it.

Bring your story close to home – even if it takes place far away from home.

Take Them on a Journey

In 1961, JFK's Secretary of Interior, Stewart Udall, discovered the stunning beauty of the Canyonlands and Colorado Plateau. This area was in the midst of a controversy regarding conservation designation, so he took a group of thirty congressmen to see it for themselves. They flew over the area, then floated on the Colorado River. In 1964, Canyonlands became a national park.

We rarely have the luxury of physically taking decision-makers to a place, so we have to rely on storytelling. How can we help our audience to experience the very thing you want them to understand?

On the brownfield cleanup project mentioned earlier, we used video to walk through a contaminated site. It showed community members that what looked to be natural wonders were really toxic and unsafe. They needed to be cleared and cleaned up to get to the end result, or happy ending, of a natural waterfront park accessible to the public.

Journeys and experiences like this aren't limited to visuals. You can still use words to paint a picture so vivid it's as though they are experiencing it. Because when they do, they are far more likely to be convinced to help.

Zoom Out

This is the crescendo moment. If you were the conductor of a symphony orchestra, you'd whip the audience into a frenzy with a booming finale to your pièce de résistance. How can you do that with the story you are drafting?

You might elevate the topic from a localized individual to a societal level. The little girl learning to play the fiddle funded by your music grant is sweet, and so is the accompanying image you have of her in the recital. But this isn't a story about teaching children to play the fiddle, you might say. It is about exposing students to experiences that build their self-confidence. If they develop a love for music along the way, that's great. Maybe you have some statistics or a study about self-confidence in young children and how to break the negative cycle. Show a world where children have self-confidence and what that means.

In other words, take your story further and higher by asking yourself what it means when...

> Show up, write your heart out, put everything you know into the piece.

What does it mean when we give kids the opportunity to learn to fiddle? They gain self-confidence, you say. And what does that mean? Well, studies show they become more likely to graduate from high school... and so on. Tie your story into why someone should care. It makes the community a safer and more thriving community.

YOUR JOURNEY

Every story should give your audience their next steps. Don't make them work for it. What should they do next? Should they click here to learn more? Get involved here? Donate? Send a letter to their civic leaders? Your story has a clear objective; it's why you've created it. Don't miss the opportunity to ask them directly to do what you hope they will do.

Show up, write your heart out, put everything you know into the piece. Don't judge yourself or the work. You've done it. The SFD is the hard part. Let's clean it up now. Ready?

LEVEL UP

REFINE

"When do I notice the editing? When it's bad."

– Craig McKay, Oscar-nominated editor for
Reds and The Silence of the Lambs

"Write drunk, edit sober." This quote is often attributed to Ernest Hemingway, but we don't know who actually said it. I added it because it describes two different states – writing and editing. I rarely do them in one sitting. And I rarely do either drunk, but you won't catch me judging. Whatever it takes to get the work done!

I prefer to sleep on a draft before I begin editing, but sometimes deadlines don't allow for that, and a few hours break will have to do. I'm not a procrastinator when creating content, so I give myself time between draft and final, which significantly reduces my self-loathing quotient. Like leaving a steak to marinate, it just needs time for ideas to meld and your brain to take a rest. When you sit down later with a fresh take, you can shape it into something you'll be proud of.

If I'm allowed a favorite part in the storytelling process, it's revising and shaping the material. Once I have a big block of material on a page, the hard work has been done: the research, the interviews, the torture of creating the first draft. All that stuff is complete. Everything I want is on the page. I persevered through the self-loathing that accompanies creating my SFD. I am still showing up. Now it's time to level up.

Doing a thorough edit on your story is vital to its success. Look at Oscar-winning films as an indicator. Since 1934, when best editing became a category, two-thirds of all Best Picture winners also won

Best Editing. To be specific, according to *Variety* magazine only nine films have won the best picture award *without* at least a nomination for editing (Dimond, 2013).

Editing makes your content a winner.

Editing makes your content a winner.

Now that you have poured your heart and soul out onto a piece of paper or screen, it's time to rework the material like a sculptor, removing unneeded material, organizing, and shaping it into its final form until it becomes something you are ready to put out into the world. A story that will compel your audience to act.

I go through my content on several passes, asking different questions at each stage. I look for different things, focussing on fat, form and flow. I won't talk about grammar here. Install an app like Grammarly or find someone to help if you're terrible at it. My husband runs any important communications through me before hitting send because he knows his grammar is awful.

Here is what I look for in no particular order.

TRIM THE FAT

Like the sculptor, remove any material that doesn't serve the finished product.

I like to be economical with my words because I respect that people don't have much time. But I also think you can say a lot with less. For that reason, I check to make sure everything in the story plays a role.

Questions to ask:

- What's my point?
- What does my audience need to know to understand it?

- Does this contribute to it? Or is it extraneous? (This is where you'll have to make some hard decisions. There will be things you want to say, and you will want to let all that crazy out onto the floor. Just as I did with Patrick when I grossly overshared on that early dinner date.)

You will need your good friend, discipline. Remember that each story is like a layer we peel back to show who we are. Keep the message simple enough for someone to engage with it and then give them opportunities to learn more. Put that other thing you really want to say somewhere else and let them know where to find it, perhaps through a hyperlink to a deeper article. Or it might be through a follow-up email. We'll talk about leveraging stories across multiple media channels before I close out the book. Jump ahead to that chapter now if you are eager to know, but I need to keep this section simple and streamlined. See what I did there?

Ask yourself if each word (and I mean word) is relevant and adds value to your message. If we don't need to know exactly what day of the week it was, leave it out. If we don't need to know how many people were at the event, leave it out. Be ruthless with your delete button.

I like to pretend I have a word count, whether I do or not. Make sure each word serves a purpose, and if you can combine several words into one meaningful word, do it. Read every word with a critical ear and eye.

But don't delete too much.

Find the Right Balance of Specificity

The other day (notice I didn't give a specific date or time), I was telling my friends about the time my husband and I temporarily lost each other on a mountain bike trail. I found myself trying to describe where I was and where he must have turned off the trail. As I tried to describe the exact curve, I stopped. It didn't matter where I was; what mattered was that he turned, and I didn't. We got lost. Pausing to think saved my friends the tedium of describing the exact tree where it happened.

Tedious, frustrating. These are not words you want to be associated with your stories. But when you insist on getting too specific, you bore your audience. And we are leveling up our stories away from boredom.

Give enough detail that people can visualize the situation. They should have sufficient information to understand and make sense of things but don't overwhelm them with tedious details. This is the balance you'll have to strike.

How do you know you're too specific?

You're too specific if you're killing people with details they don't need, such as where my husband and I lost each other on the trail. Keep coming back to the questions above and ask – does this contribute to the point, or is it extraneous?

How do you know you're too generic?

Words like *world-class*, *amazing*, and *incredible* mean any number of things to any number of people. And that tells you they don't mean much at all. Catching yourself using any of these words is a hint that you are too generic. A great exercise I use is the five-year-old kid drill: Ask, "Why is it so amazing?" "But, why?" "But, why?" Maybe the third or fourth time of asking will give you the right answer. Use that.

Verbs like *do, be* (I am, he is) and *said*. Stop and ask how you can express this better? Are there more active and descriptive verbs?

The most recent Oxford dictionary contains 171,000 words. The average American knows anywhere from 20,000 to 40,000 words. That's how many words we *know,* not how many we actually *use.* It's safe to say that, on average, we use less than twenty percent of our beautiful language, meaning that we rely on our regular stable of words. I like to make a game by extending my vocabulary and broadening the range of words available for my stories.

I do this by paying attention when I read. For example, I'll come across a word like symptomatic and think, "Hey, there's a word I never use." Then, I'll be editing something and come across a sentence I had drafted: "It's indicative of a bigger, more prevailing philosophy." Replace it with the word symptomatic. One word to replace seven. See? Words are fun!

Make sure that every word serves a purpose.

> Make sure that every word serves a purpose.

Beginner's Mind

Would you ever start a Netflix series at Episode Six? Usually not. It's easiest to start from the pilot and progress from there. If you start in the middle, you end up trying to figure out who the characters are and what is going on. This might be OK for a popular show with eye candy and movie stars, but our job is to make things easy for your audience. If we make them work too hard, they'll lose interest or get easily distracted.

As the storyteller of your organization, you don't have the luxury of sequencing your stories. That complicates matters because until now, we've been discussing using different stories for different objectives – from awareness to trust to action. But you don't necessarily have control over who is seeing which story at what time.

Don't assume your audience has been following everything you've been creating. Thinking you've already posted about Johnny on Facebook doesn't mean everyone saw it. So when you do a follow-up post, a brief explanation will be in order.

With that in mind, I always like to review my draft with a beginner's mind. Would someone new understand what is going on? If this isn't your pilot episode, how can you link the audience (either literally or figuratively) to the first story. How can you eliminate that Episode Six confusion?

Avoid jargon if possible, and if you can't, then explain. Acronyms should always be clarified. Again, don't assume anything.

Are you worried that you don't know what others know or don't know? Ask an outsider to review your work before hitting publish. What questions do they have? Does it all make sense?

Ask yourself: Would a beginner understand this?

FORM

The last consideration in leveling up stories is the voice, vocabulary and consistency. Like a brand's visual identity, a story should feel similar every time. We wouldn't have a corporate, formal voice in one piece and another loaded with slang. The way people experience your organization is part of your brand, and it's good to be intentional about how you come across. You've considered this if you've done the planning process when you discussed how you want to be perceived. Whether it's to be a trusted and non-partisan resource, a break from all the serious news, or a hallowed institution, these decide how you will communicate and what your voice will be from casual to formal.

This decision will dictate the language you use, but I always argue for being conversational in your stories. If you wouldn't say it out loud, don't say it in your stories.

A few final words on making your voice more powerful and compelling.

Active voice vs. passive voice. According to Grammarly, "active voice means that a sentence has a subject that acts upon its verb. Passive voice means that a subject is a recipient of a verb's action."

A quick giveaway that you are using passive voice is a verb ending with -ing. "I was using a pen rather than a pencil", or "I used a pen rather than a pencil". The second is stronger here, but not always! Sometimes the passive voice just works better. I suggest that if you find a passive statement, do the exercise to make it active and compare. Then choose. Rules are useful until they aren't. I am less concerned about the rules and more concerned about creating a compelling story that is a pleasure to read.

Jazz Up the Language

I like to review my use of vocabulary and replace boring or lazy words with more descriptive words. Here's an example from a client's speech, where the point was to show how storytelling had made a previously unremarkable brand trendy.

The first draft: "Now, it's trendy to wear these boots. People pay a premium to wear Red Wings with leggings and oversized flannel shirts from Pendleton."

In my review, I felt we could combine a few things and describe "people" more vividly, so I wrote. "Now, fashionistas pay top dollar at trendy shops to wear Red Wings paired with leggings and oversized Pendleton plaid shirts."

See the difference? Instead of people, they are fashionistas. A generic term made more specific, maybe a bit more concise and descriptive.

Every sentence matters, so don't take a single one for granted. You, however, are covering topics with more gravity than Red Wings. In being economical and more descriptive with your words, you are more powerful. Doing a better job of conveying your message means a better job at getting people to care about your thing.

Jazz Up the Language Without Jacking It Up

In the example above, the words became more specific and descriptive. In many cases, I see so-called storytellers get excited to use big twenty-five-cent words. They sound really impressive, but leave the audience wondering what the hell they just read. Take this merger announcement between two mega tech companies.

"For our users, the new <merged companies> will offer best-in-class capabilities across a much larger combined portfolio – immediately increasing choice and value while featuring the scale, resources and world-class talent required to accelerate innovation and address future needs."

I have no idea what this means. Do you? This announcement was a missed opportunity to describe how the merger will impact existing subscribers by providing scenarios and specifics. But they didn't. They assumed their impressive language was enough to satisfy.

Humans communicate through stories, and organizations are humans doing business with humans. I implore you to engage in the currency of conversation and turn these crazy sentences into something meaningful.

FLOW

We are not in the business of creating literary masterpieces, but we do want to take our audience on a journey. We want to give them an experience, so your stories should be easy and even a pleasure to read regardless of the topic. I say this understanding that you are often writing about difficult topics such as violence and abuse. Please understand that when I say *easy* and *pleasurable*, I don't mean we give people beach reading. I simply mean we don't want to make them work hard to follow the story. It should flow well.

> Your stories should be easy and even a pleasure to read regardless of the topic

Have you revealed details in a way that unfolds one step at a time? Bring your beginner's mind to ensure your audience has what they need before they read each sentence. Even if the story is a social post and is only a few sentences long, order and flow are critical to the consumption, understanding and engagement with your story.

What does your first sentence look or sound like? Is it intriguing enough to pull your audience in?

A Clash of Cymbals Marks the Beginning

Take a close look at where you started your story and consider how or if it might be better. Go through your draft and find something that is attractive. (Attractive, as in magnetic. It pulls you in.) Don't feel you have to tell a story in chronological order. Maybe there is a turning point, or a quote, or a surprising statistic you'd like to lead with and back off from there to bring your audience to that point. Can you be mysterious or foreshadowing?

This brings us to transitions. In longer-form writing, it's a great idea to help your audience along on their journey, so remind them, occasionally, where you are and where you are going.

In general, reading aloud helps with all these things because you can often hear where something doesn't resonate better than when you are reading it silently.

The Crescendo Ending

Start with a clash of cymbals to get their attention and end with a bang. Your ending could serve several purposes: summarizing, drawing conclusions, and identifying the next steps (or a call to action).

Summarizing is important because it takes everything you've stated and distills it into something memorable. The crescendo effect often happens when you elevate the conversation and answer the question, "What is this really about?" The answer is typically a happy ending. It might be an idealistic or unattainable happy ending, but it's something your audience can imagine and be hopeful for.

Your objective is to get people on board with your idea, and in most cases, that means ending on an optimistic note. Something like, "We can make a difference, and here is how." Then you tell them what's next. "We need you to show up, sign this, share this, learn more here, consider giving."

YOUR JOURNEY

There's a lot to think about when distilling your research, notes and interviews into a story. It's like the game of golf – with which I have a love-hate relationship. If you worry about everything you were taught, you will slice the ball into the woods. Instead, remember the foundational bits. My coach told me to focus on the backswing and the follow-through when I step up to the tee, and everything else will fall into place.

So, I suggest you focus on showing up and leveling up and everything will fall into place if you've done the foundational work. You've done the planning, and you understand the power of storytelling. You've asked the right questions based on your objectives, and now you have the material to work with. Show up and level up, and it will fall into place. Golf is as frustrating as hell, but when you hit the ball just right and watch it sail down the fairway, the rewards keep you coming back for more.

Read aloud to highlight any speed bumps in your stories. These gaps or statements stop the easy flow, and you'll catch them more easily when read aloud.

Questions to ask:

1. Can I be more concise with descriptive words?

_____

_____

_____

2. Am I using jargon that my audience won't understand, or can I replace it with something more interesting and conversational?

_____

_____

_____

3. Am I using words that don't mean anything, such as; amazing, world-class, synergistic. Use words that have meaning.

_____

_____

_____

And now (gulp), it's time to put your work out into the world.

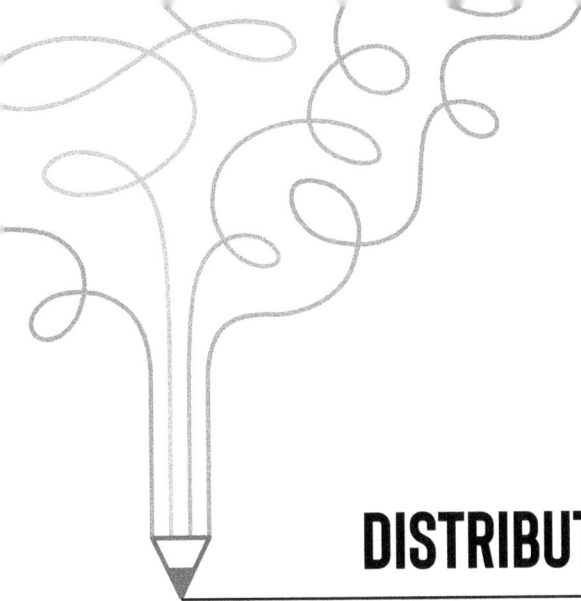

DISTRIBUTE

There's this thing that happens when my husband starts a sentence, out of the blue, with a "Soooooo....." in such a way that I know something big is coming. Something that requires me to brace myself. In my mind, I grab onto my big girl pants and yank them up in preparation for whatever bombshell or disappointment is about to be delivered.

It's time to hike up your big girl pants because your story is about to get released to the public, and when you do that, you step out of the arena and onto the stage. This is good. You are amazing for doing this. But you also set yourself up for, gasp, "feedback".

That is why this section will help you create your circle, filter the feedback and build your defenses. It will address other hurdles that keep you the world's best-kept secret in the land of invisibility. We're going to talk about your issues with perfection and your fear of feedback.

And finally, I want to help you make the

You'll learn that people aren't paying that close attention to you, and repetition is your friend.

most of every story. Don't be afraid to re-use and repeat them. You'll learn that people aren't paying that close attention to you, and repetition is your friend.

You've come a long way to get here, my friend, and it's time to Distribute – to tell your story.

PROCESS

*"There are two spiritual dangers in not owning
a farm. One is the danger of supposing that
breakfast comes from the grocery, and the
other that heat comes from the furnace.*

*"To avoid the first danger, one should
plant a garden, preferably where there
is no grocer to confuse the issue.*

*"To avoid the second, he should lay a split of
good oak on the andirons, preferably where
there is no furnace, and let it warm his shins
while a February blizzard tosses the trees
outside. If one has cut, split, hauled, and
piled his own good oak, and let his mind
work the while, he will remember much
about where the heat comes from, and with
a wealth of detail denied to those who spend
the weekend in town astride a radiator."*

– Aldo Leopold (Leopold, 1968).

You have planned, researched, interviewed, created, edited and finalized a story to compel your audience to think or do something differently, to get them to care about your thing.

You've identified the objective and your audience. You've gathered the material – the stories, data, and facts, and put it into a structure that feels organized while tugging on your readers' emotional heartstrings. You've run it through several filters to ensure it flows and has enough information without overwhelming details. This process might have taken you thirty minutes for a social post or weeks for an in-depth report.

You have gone from enthusiasm as you embark on a meaningful project to diligence as you gather materials and self-loathing as you create a draft and have the discipline to polish it. Needless to say, it's been a ride.

You've planted a garden where there is no grocer and perhaps put some wood on the andirons before it gets too cold.

Then, Someone shows up and stomps on your garden and extinguishes your fire. That Someone crushes puppy souls, has a better idea or knows more than you. This person has an opinion and a voice that (they feel) must be heard. They drag out meetings because they have vital input, while the rest of the group wrings their hands with impatience outside the frame of the Zoom webcam.

This chapter is about That Someone and managing your creative and approval processes to prevent them from sabotaging your efforts.

You were out in the forest chopping wood while the people who review your work were standing by the radiator in town. It's easy enough for them to provide input, but you will have to manage the process.

There are three different potential attacks from the people who stand on your sidelines:

1. Your team during the creation process. Fix it by creating your circle.

2. Your team during the approval process. Fix them by filtering the feedback.

3. Critics in your audience. Silence them by building your defense.

Here we go.

CREATE YOUR CIRCLE

A news anchor has a team. No one does this work single-handedly. The size of your team will depend on your resources. You'll need reporters, writers, maybe a videographer, photographer, an editor, and your review team.

I'll leave it to you to decide how many of each you'll need. In some cases, one person will have multiple roles. If you are a small organization, you might be the reporter, photographer and editor. Your executive director or colleague might be your second pair of eyes (the editor). Someone on your board might have a communications background and be willing to review everything.

Create your circle and be clear on everyone's roles.

Your reporter(s) are in the field capturing the stories. This might be you, or it could be field staff or volunteers. The closer reporters can get to the front lines of the work, the better.

They might refer interesting story sources and ideas to you or do the interviews themselves. Or they might create the story and then turn it over to you. To get the most success, define these boundaries before you start.

A note on getting your reporters engaged: If you're having a difficult time, make sure you've communicated the importance of storytelling. Use the first few chapters of this book to make your case for storytelling. Find your ambassadors. Not everyone will be willing, and that's OK. Consider using this skill or work as part of the job description when bringing new members onto your team. Knowing from the start that storytelling is part of the job might shape your selection process.

Your videographer and photographer might be someone with an iPhone or more sophisticated with full-on professional equipment. Again, depending on your resources and the particular story you are working on, you'll know which end of the spectrum you should be on. Remember that your videos and photos do not always have to be professional-grade, but they should be quality. You can find loads of tips and hacks for creating good quality videos online. You can get your stories out without breaking the bank with some basic knowledge about audio, lighting, and camera angles.

Editors. Who will be reviewing the work, and what does the approval process look like? Without exception, my clients who have a clear and assertive approach to getting the work approved have the most successful storytelling efforts. This is critical because having too many people in the kitchen will dilute your message. Everyone feels they have to contribute, and when you try to please everyone, you do yourself a disservice.

Questions to ask:

- Who is on your team, and what are their roles?

- Who do you want to be involved in the creative process? You know who the difficult people are in your group. Some people collaborate well and provide constructive input, while others detract from the process. Know who should be involved early on.

I want you to get your thing out into the world relatively unscathed by committee compromise. So, be intentional about who is part of your process, communicate that upfront, then be ready to filter the feedback.

FILTER THE FEEDBACK

Feedback, for the most part, should be like receiving a suggestion, not a demand. I get that there are exceptions to this rule. A client concerned about their privacy, your boss, or a large donor might have input you cannot say no to. With those exceptions in mind, when appropriate, consider feedback as a suggestion.

We receive feedback from different people differently, and I know certain people in your process will bristle your feathers, regardless of the input. Try to look past this. Ignore the fact that they could have offered this input in a more respectful tone. I know that people don't have the best communication skills. It's why I have a job – and possibly why you do too.

Take a deep breath and set your ego aside.

> Take a deep breath and set your ego aside.

The important point to consider is when the feedback elevates the work and when it starts to compromise it. Understand the difference between input that is semantic or genuinely making a better point. Maybe someone suggested you soften language that is rather direct and might get you into trouble. Are they compromising your point or protecting you? A good conversation is needed, and it starts with you understanding why the suggestion was made.

Questions to ask:

- Does the input make the work better?

- Does it protect or expose us?
- Does it align with the objective?
- Does it reach our audience emotionally?
- How does it affect other elements later in the piece?

If you aren't satisfied with the responses to these reflections, then, hopefully, you are empowered to thank them for the advice and ignore it, although you might have to rationalize.

I recently did this with a client who suggested a change that I thought about overnight. We were working on key messaging for their newly rebranded healthcare clinic. The draft focused on whole health for your whole life, and she thought it might be more impactful to focus on patient-centered care.

This idea didn't resonate with me, but it wasn't enough to just say I didn't like it. I questioned my thought process. (It's OK to challenge your own thinking.) Was I operating in a vacuum? What if we did go with her suggested change?

Here is where I landed, and I share my email message to inspire you to engage in conversation around the problem. Do so without a right or wrong attitude because there typically isn't a right or wrong answer. Taking the time to explore why you don't think it's the right way to proceed can be a valuable exercise.

> Hi <first name>
>
> I've been giving this some thought as to why the patient-centered tagline doesn't resonate for me.
>
> Here is where I landed. :) The "centered around you messages" feel editorialized. For example, from your audience

perspective: I don't trust you telling me the experience is centered around me. I need to hear that from others.

Instead, when you tell me I can find whole health for my whole life, that means something to me. This is factual, the other is subjective. This is more significant also: what matters more to me, as your potential patient for life is that you are going to give me whole health for my whole life, - not that everything will be centered around me.

Having said that, you could shop it around and see what others think?

Another thought I had is that your ads could feature messages like the patient-centered process. More of an ad message than a tagline message.

What does that bring up for you? What do you think?

The client replied in complete agreement. You might not get a similar response, but we came to a compromise because I didn't knock her idea. I suggested shopping it around to the target audience in case she felt uncertain. (We didn't end up doing that because she did agree.)

The approval process will challenge you on several levels. It's wise to enter this with an open mind. Set your ego aside and be self-aware, knowing you don't know everything. You are not your work, so don't take the feedback personally.

On the other hand, you'll need to have the confidence to protect your baby if you feel it's being sabotaged by bad advice with good intentions. Just like protecting your family, be ready to defend the work in a respectful way. Be the proud parent standing up for your kid that maybe someone doesn't totally understand.

BUILD YOUR DEFENSE

You are a purpose-driven leader working hard to implement change. But people resist change and take issue with how you make it. The work you do will open you to criticism. And when we put ourselves out there, we are on the front line of what sometimes feels like a really mean dodgeball game or worse.

The best way to prepare for this possible or eventual pummeling is to do what any political candidate does when preparing for a debate: Know what the arguments will be and design your own answers and talking points.

I always like to play devil's advocate before we hit the "send" button by asking what could go wrong. Play out those scenarios and prepare accordingly. It might mean you change the way you word something (proactively). It might mean you have some responses or talking points prepared in response (reactively).

When we videoed the story of how the brownfield cleanup would create a natural waterfront park and provide more precious public access to the lake, the city planner we interviewed said that this property "could have been developed into high-end home sites". But it wasn't – the community was saving it. While the development was a compelling argument, it had been proposed before, and the community was outraged by the idea. Even mentioning it in the video would be a trigger, so why say anything at all? Why not just leave it as a happy ending, which is more precious access to the waterfront. We edited out the mention.

Yet when we prepared to announce the new name of the animal welfare organization, we knew there would be backlash on social media on the topic of animals in cages and whether there should or shouldn't be at the "shelter". Rather than alter the message, the client created a series of responses and talking points for the social media manager to handle. In this way, they could respond individually if the concern arose (and others would see it) rather than let that drive the message.

Having your defense mechanism in place makes you look good as an organization. It minimizes the backlash and, best of all, it does wonders for the morale of staff who are armed with what they need to defend the work you are all doing together.

Good process is good protection.

YOUR JOURNEY

Good process is good protection. It protects you from personal insult, it protects your work from compromise by committee, and it protects your organization by building a strong defense.

Now, as the news anchor, you become the face of your organization as the stories your team has crafted are presented. You will be challenged on your storytelling journey. Having your circle of support, filtering your feedback and building your defenses will enable you to cut through the noise.

But you're still hovering over the "send" button. I see you there; eyes squinted shut, nose crinkled up, cursor hovering. You're overthinking it and worried it's not ready yet.

Next up: how your pursuit of perfection could be holding you back.

MOMENTUM

"It is not the critic who counts; not the man who points out how the strong man stumbles or where the doer of deeds could have done them better. The credit belongs to the man who is actually in the arena..."

– Theodore Roosevelt.

It happens to all of us – that vulnerable moment when it's time to put your work out for others to see. You wonder how it will be received. Will you be criticized? Are you taking a stand for something that will generate a backlash? Will this thing you've created achieve what you hope?

I want to address the hurdles – those things that create inertia. It's comfortable enough to sit in your office, creating beautiful ideas, but until you get them out there, nothing is going to happen.

IN PURSUIT OF PERFECTION

In mountain biking, it's common knowledge that momentum is your friend. If you come upon rocks or tree roots on the trail and slow down out of concern or fear, you will more than likely go over your front tire. That's known as an "endo" – I think it's short for end-over-head. It's not much fun, and you won't get to your destination in one piece if you keep it up. You need to pedal through that stuff because momentum is your friend.

At the outset of the COVID pandemic, a pharmacy client shot a great video inside their retail space answering the questions, fears and concerns on people's minds. He suggested ways to fortify our immune systems, showcasing the items he was talking about. He even showed us around the rest of the store, which had recently been renovated. But this was weeks after lockdown, and it didn't feel appropriate to talk about hardware in a story about staying healthy during the lockdown. We kept the message focused on what really mattered. What did feel right was to talk about naturopathic ways to boost your immune system (with the beautiful renovation in the background speaking for itself).

I loved the video because it came from the owner, who was knowledgeable and looked straight into the camera while he calmly gave valuable information. He established trust and made me want to call in or order whatever he suggested. It was short, high quality, and filmed on an iPhone.

I said, ""I love it, publish it!" But they came back with many questions:

- What about a video intro/outro graphic? Should we have one done?
- How long do we want each of these videos to be?
- What is our publishing schedule?
- Should we buy lighting and a better camera?

And ten more questions I won't include here.

Don't allow overthinking to hold up putting your ideas out into the world. Systems, processes and better tools are great, but they can also serve as procrastination and inertia to your momentum.

Later that week, another client sent through an article he wanted to share socially. Again, I told him to go ahead, but he wanted to wait to have a social media strategy in place.

Don't get me wrong, planning is good. But there is a balance between figuring out all the details of something and just getting it out there so you can iterate and improve. Maybe no one will like the videos, the product, or the podcast you are trying to launch. Perhaps you'll get some feedback and modify it accordingly.

The tech community has a term for this kind of thing: it's the minimally viable product. Build something useful and get it out there for others to play with and comment on so you can continually iterate and make it better.

Slack didn't launch a perfect product when they went out to market (Butterfield, 2014). They put out a minimally viable product and let their users help drive progress from there. Instagram looked very different when it first launched than it does now. They've slowly rolled out features and interface improvements. You are surrounded by this every day, and you and your organization are no exception.

"But wait," you might be saying, "we don't want to put something out that isn't a polished reflection of who we are!" To which I respond, get over yourself. In the words of leadership expert and author Matt Church, "people aren't paying that close attention to you" (Church, 2021). Well, it's true, and they definitely won't be paying attention if you aren't putting anything out there because you're waiting to get a system in place or buy a better light.

EYE ON THE OBJECTIVE

The other thing about mountain biking is that if you stare at the very thing you want to avoid, like the rock on the trail, you will crash into it. Instead, pedal the bike (maintain your momentum) and look ahead, focusing on where you want to go. Alternate your vision between just ahead of your tire (or what is directly in front of you) and the line you want to ride (your objective).

My Advice: That podcast can launch without the perfect name

Srinivas Rao is the host of *The Unmistakable Creative* podcast. Originally launched as *Blogcast FM*, it ran under that name for years with tens of thousands of listeners before he rebranded. It was the content, not the name, that drew people in. Of course, with the rebrand, he grew even further (Rao, n.d.). My point is that your video can go out now, on the understanding that the series will be upgraded as you progress. Get started. Put your work out there. Iterate.

> Get started. Put your work out there. Iterate.

The best-laid plans never go as expected, anyway. Don't hold things up for the plan you keep meaning to develop.

These details are rocks in the trail, and you shouldn't be looking at them. Pedal through the obstacles, and you'll make it to the other side a better rider than before.

I'm tempted to end the chapter here, but I think there's one more obstacle you can't take your eyes off. And it's holding you back.

FEAR OF FEEDBACK

There you are, ready to hit the send button, and what's running through your mind? Is there a typo? Will it go viral? What will people think? Will they realize I don't know what I'm talking about? Will they disagree? Is there anything here that is going to infuriate people?

These will hold you back, and you know intuitively if these concerns are valid or in your head. Since you've made it this far with my advice (particularly in the Process chapter), I'm going to proceed on the assumption that the concerns are in your head.

FROM SO WHAT? TO SO FUNDED!

I do my best to separate myself from my work. I know this is much easier said than done, but it's important not to take the feedback personally. You are not your work. If someone takes issue with something you've created, that's good. You've made them feel something.

A listener to my podcast, *Breaking Trail,* called to rant about a recent episode. I know this person (which is why they had my phone number), and as I listened to him rage about why he hated the episode, a few thoughts flashed through my brain. It looked like this:

> *Ah, Lisa, you idiot, you knew you shouldn't have published that episode. What were you thinking?*
>
> *No, you were right to publish it. Now, tell this person all the reasons why you were right.*
>
> *Instead, when he finished, I laughed. I laughed not to diminish his feelings but to say, "I get it. I know how frustrating hearing that must have been. Thank you for sharing your feedback."*
>
> *To which he responded, "Thank you. I feel so much better now."*

Our instinct is to react, while most people just want to be heard or seen. The rest are either trolls or have valid points.

Your Reaction is More Important than the Infraction

You might get a hundred positive comments, but the two that are negative stick with you. Now, what to do?

Knowing when to engage, apologize, and update something that is incorrect will be key. You are more often judged on how you handle the situation than on the situation itself.

In considering how to react to negative feedback, I often look ahead to my destination, to the outcome I desire. This prevents the automatic response of replying in anger or defense – which never works. It helps to pause, even sleep on it if that is appropriate.

I could write an entire book on this topic, but it ventures outside the scope of this one, so I'll keep it brief.

Sometimes you might have deserved the negative reaction – perhaps something slipped through the cracks, and you are in the wrong. At other times, you didn't deserve it; someone might have it out for you or were just downright unfair. You may or may not be able to turn the person in question. If the reaction is public, consider that people are watching and want to see how you handle the situation.

Importantly, we want to defuse the situation, not inflame it. Acting in any way that aggravates is a mistake. For example, if the person wrote a long-winded saga with every detail, don't feel the need to honor it with a detailed point-by-point response. We want to remain calm and put this baby to sleep fast. If appropriate, offer to continue the conversation privately.

Show empathy. Make it clear that you understand how disappointing or upsetting the situation must have been. Most people just want to be heard.

Say sorry if you owe them an apology.

Thank the commenter, if appropriate. Getting constructive feedback makes your organization better.

Know when to stop engaging. Say your piece, and move on. Hopefully, others in your community will come to your defense. If you ignore the trolls, they will eventually go away because it's no fun when they aren't getting any reaction.

Whatever you do, never respond in anger or with emotion.

Don't let the fear of feedback hold you back. A client once said to me, "If you stop and kick every barking dog, you'll never get anywhere." (By the way, I'd never kick a dog, but I thought the expression worked.) You can't be everything to everyone.

> Don't let the fear of feedback hold you back.

YOUR JOURNEY

Remember, it's not the critic who counts. It is the person in the arena doing the work and getting their ass kicked that matters.

Love it, or hate it, but don't be ambivalent. Remember that you are stepping into the arena and you matter. Your idea of change matters.

Our pursuit of perfection and fear of feedback are the greatest hurdles (and the most excellent invitations to procrastination).

What have you been holding onto, worried about putting out into the world?

LEVERAGE

"Leverage is a term used most often metaphorically. Its origin is in physics, where a lever literally 'amplifies an input force to provide a greater output force.' In all other contexts, we're seeking figurative levers to pull which will magnify the impact of our actions."

– Col Fink (Fink, 2021).

By now, you've realized this storytelling thing isn't a shortcut to getting your idea of change to happen. There is no formula, although there are structures. It's not a "get rich quick" scheme, nor is it a trick to get people to believe something that is not true. Good storytelling comes from the heart, but it also takes a mix of strategic thinking, creative thinking, listening skills and a fair dose of intuition.

Storytelling takes more time and energy than not telling a story. Your to-do list might include items like "year-end fundraising campaign copy" or "annual report content" and it's not as simple as ticking the checkbox and writing something from the top of your head. You have to do a lot of planning, research and interviewing before you even sit down in front of your blank screen.

But here is where it gets good, because storytelling ultimately saves you time and exponentially increases your return.

All this effort amplifies to create a greater output force. In the blog post mentioned above, Col Fink mentions other uses of leverage. In the world of finance, when you profit from borrowed money, you are "leveraged". In software as a service (SaaS), you leverage passive income from a single product.

Leveraging storytelling makes it an awesome tool. You can turn those stories to multiple uses, saving time and allowing yourself to be more effective with messaging more quickly.

What if you engaged in a cadence of story gathering and storing for over a year and entered these stories into a database with appropriate tags so they could be easily retrieved? You would have rich content to draw upon when needed.

Input from these stories gives you greater understanding of what you should be talking about. Rather than scrambling for something to say in your next project, you will find yourself brimming with content.

In December 2020, the Education Alliance asked me to craft a letter from the Executive Director for an end-of-year recap to donors. We wanted the letter to show that despite the pandemic and closed schools, the client adapted quickly and directed funds to effective use. Nothing went to waste. We could have just said it, but we wanted to show it. Show, don't tell.

Earlier in the year, I had interviewed grant recipients for the annual report. The full stories ran in the client's blog, while shorter "snack" stories were shared on social media with links to the full blog. Three of the stories ran in the annual report.

When sitting down to write the cover letter, I reviewed those stories that I had spent hours gathering and identified a theme that tied in with the letter's objective. I pulled out three examples and distilled each to a single sentence. Every story included a character, a conflict and a resolution.

When we generalize and over-use common words, we fail to understand what they mean. The stories came to life with real people and real problems solved. The conversation then went beyond issues to talk about what they mean for society, answering the question: Why does it matter?

I sent the draft to the Executive Director for approval, and she wrote back that it brought tears to her eyes. That year, they had the largest year-end campaign on record.

MAKE EACH STORY COUNT

Let's explore how this might look for you in the coming year. You'll start the plan by identifying your objectives. You will have a few. They might include raising awareness, shifting perception, influencing actions, or raising money through large gifts, grants, or individual donors.

Use the five questions in the Plan chapter to identify the main stories you want to capture. Commit to talking to someone at least once a month. The people you speak to could be founders, board members, donors, clients, civic or business leaders, third-party experts. Make sure to get a diverse set of interviews.

Plan each interview for multiple purposes. Get more material than you need. Maybe you'll capture the interview on video so you can re-use snippets of the video or audio. Snap photos and get a tour of the physical space if appropriate to the story.

Develop a system to tag, title and file your story assets so that you can retrieve them easily. This might feel like overkill in the first few months, but trust me, it will save time later. Use the spreadsheet started for your plan to identify the media you will use and the different tags that fit the interviews.

From one interview, you might get enough content to write multiple blogs on a variety of topics. Remember, don't cram everything into one! The accompanying video and images can be used on social media. Add meaningful quotes to your spreadsheet or a list for use in email campaigns and donor appeals.

Consider investing in a videographer if you don't have one on staff and get them to come with you on several of these interviews. After a few months, they can edit together a great video for your gala. At the end of the year, review your stories and choose highlights for the annual report. Identify the umbrella story – the "what's this all about" and bingo! You have your cover letter from the President or Executive Director.

A sustained and intentional process of story gathering allows you to pull from great content and aggregate it into a theme on demand.

You may have heard the legend (I can't find any actual evidence) of Picasso selling a napkin doodle for a large sum of money. There are many versions of this story, and some even argue it was a different artist, James McNeill Whistler, but the point of the story remains.

A woman approached Picasso in a restaurant and asked him to draw something on a napkin. When she asked for it, he offered it to her for ten thousand francs. Astounded, she cried, "It only took you thirty seconds to do the drawing!" "In fact", he said, "it took me a lifetime to be able to do this drawing in thirty seconds."

Without comparing myself to Picasso, it might have only taken me thirty minutes to write that letter for the Executive Director, but it took years of storytelling experience and hours of prior research to get there.

MEASURING OUTCOMES

Entire books have been written on the topic of measurement, so I refer you to experts such as Johna Burke of AMEC, Shonali Burke (no relation), and even Avinash Kaushik if you want to really geek out.

And because so many books have been dedicated to the subject, it's hard to do it justice here. But I would be remiss if I didn't talk about the importance of tracking and measuring because inevitably, your Board, your boss, a donor, someone will ask why you are devoting so much time and effort to storytelling, and I want you to be able to respond.

So I'm going to give you a baseline plan.

In the Plan chapter, I gave you a brief framework for selecting metrics. I like to base metrics on the audience journey.

- Awareness. How big is the audience? (On whatever platform or channel you choose.)

- Perception and engagement. It's not enough to just be aware. Are they engaging, commenting, sharing, talking about you?

- Action. Are they volunteering, showing up, giving?

This is just a start. As Johna Burke said, only looking at the numbers will mislead you more than help you.

You'll also want to measure audience response and effects, such as how reputation or opinion has changed.

Try this Scenario

An animated video created to shift perception about a tax levy gets 8,000 views in a community of 10,000 people. The levy passes by 1,200 votes. Can you credit the video for the outcome?

Burke says you need to ask: Where is the video going? Who geographically saw it? And were they talking to others about it on and offline? Were the 8,000 views unique? Adding a call to action is helpful to gather this information. Ask viewers if they are going to vote; and if they support the initiative.

It would be unfair to give all the credit for the levy passing to the video. But the outcome was positive in that the levy passed and was consistent with the messaging presented in the video. We won't take all the credit, but we did move the needle. It's impossible to know for sure without a sophisticated plan in place.

The AMEC framework mentioned in Chapter Two provides a structure to understand, attribute and create actionable results. Their interactive framework is free to use and includes an in-depth tutorial. For more information, go to AMEC.org/amecframework.

A client tracked giving year over year once they began their storytelling efforts. They saw a nine percent increase in the first year, followed by sixteen percent in the second year. That came to a total of $138,000 more than two years earlier. Before you attribute this entirely to storytelling efforts, many other factors come into play. How did costs compare? Did costs increase? Then adjust accordingly. It's important to understand all data points that drive the result.

- What worked?
- What didn't?
- What was the business impact?
- What have we learned so we can be successful in the future?
- Quantitative metrics are a good start.
- Qualitative measures take it further.

Short of microchipping the people in your audience and conducting brain scans, there is no hard and fast way to accurately measure your storytelling effectiveness. Depending on your resources, use polls, surveys, analytics and data, and do the best you can.

Before implementing any campaigns that matter, decide how you want to track success, as that will influence your next step or call to action. This is a great exercise because it makes you think about what you want your audience to do next – and you always want them to do something. Everything you do has a purpose. Emails should ask for a next action – to click through or call. Print ads can have unique URLs and phone numbers, while event attendance should drive email collections.

> Before implementing any campaigns that matter, decide how you want to track success, as that will influence your next step or call to action.

YOUR JOURNEY

Teams are maxed out, particularly in the nonprofit sector. Taking on new initiatives feels overwhelming. This book might even make you feel overwhelmed when my goal was to make it intuitive.

The first step is all that is needed to start progress. Start by making a list of story ideas based on the questions in the planning chapters, then schedule your first interview. You are on your way! Once you have the stories, you have the content you need, which, in the end, will save you the time you are worried about spending right now. That's your first return.

If you're small and overwhelmed, do the basic tracking I shared earlier, and show a return to your Board and your leadership. One step at a time. When you can show results, you can get more resources. Start slowly, be laser focused on who you want to reach and what you want to achieve, and build from there.

It will take a lot of time, but it will also give you time back. The investment is worth it.

AND THEY ALL LIVED
HAPPILY EVER AFTER

WHAT THIS BOOK IS REALLY ABOUT

"...people are weary of being asked to do the least they can possibly do. People are yearning to measure the full distance of their potential on behalf of the causes that they care about deeply."

– Dan Pallotta (Pallotta, 2013).

I have used plenty of words and chapters to say that stories allow your audience to connect with you. When they connect with you, they understand you, trust you, and become advocates on your behalf. They invest time in you, and they take action. They believe in your idea of change and want to join in and help make it happen.

People crave a sense of belonging. They want to know they are making a difference in the world.

This is about making a connection so you can make change.

Connection means many different things to different people and can end up not meaning anything at all, so let's explore the word and the idea as we wrap up. If I turn to the Oxford English Dictionary, connect means "to have or establish a rapport; to place or establish in relationship; to think of (something or someone) as being related to or involved with another person, thing, event, or idea" (Oxford English Dictionary, n.d.).

We want to be moved; we want to belong. We are tired of being asked to do the least we can possibly do.

I hope this book has inspired you to think about your storytelling differently. Understanding what makes stories so powerful means you don't have to think so hard about technical storytelling. In the act of asking the right questions, internally as an organization and externally of the people who will tell your stories, you are naturally doing everything I've described. You are making a connection without scheming.

A friend put her home on the market in Eastern Washington and received an offer of $100,000 below the asking price.

Rather than be offended (as I know I would be), she wrote a letter in her counteroffer. She started with, "I'd like to share with you what you get from this house outside of what you can find in the listing package." And she went on to describe what it was like when the sun rises in the morning on the front porch. She described the yard that stretched down to the lake and the activities and experiences in this home at different times of the day.

The potential buyers came back with a new offer: Increased by $90,000.

I know many of us in the nonprofit world struggle to report on ROI, but I think we can all calculate the ROI of my friend's story. A cool $90,000.

What is an emotional connection — outside of what the dictionary tells us?

My friend's letter clearly struck a chord that made an emotional connection that persuaded someone to act and removed the purchase's transactional nature. Suddenly, money wasn't the driving force, it was emotion.

Making an emotional connection isn't as hard as it sounds. Story naturally does it all. You don't even have to think about it, just like the golf swing. If you focus on your backswing and the follow-through, the rest happens. Similarly, focus on the discovery (**storylistening**), the distilling (**storycrafting**) and the distribution (**storytelling**), and the rest – the trust, understanding, and emotional connection – all fall into place.

> Making an emotional connection isn't as hard as it sounds. Story naturally does it all.

Let's return to the finish line of that trail run where my husband easily cut through the noise to get my attention and a photo of me finishing. From my perspective, all those other people merged into one big noisy marketplace. I couldn't tell one from the other. None was familiar and none had my trust.

You can share all the facts and data you want, but if you aren't cutting through the noise with stories, as far as the people you are trying to reach are concerned, you are just a part of that noisy crowd. You will go unnoticed.

On the other hand, if you take the time to create those relationships and build that trust, you will remove the transactional nature and elevate your organization to where your audience asks, "what do you need?" And there you'll find yourselves rising from So what? to So Funded!

APPENDIX

Story Worksheet

Story idea/message	Type (awareness, shift perception, trust, action)	Who to talk to	Assign story to:	Timing	Campaign or Project (ie fundraising, annual report)

LBG lisa@bigleapcreative.com lisa gerber

REFERENCES

Abel, J. & Glass, I., 2015. *Out on the Wire: The Storytelling Secrets of the New Masters of Radio*. First ed. New York: Broadway Books.

Baines, P., 2011. *Hands Across the Water*. Sydney: Macmillan Australia.

Berger, W., 2014. *A More Beautiful Question: The power of inquiry to spark breakthrough ideas*. New York: Bloomsbury.

Broder, J. M., 2013. *Stalled Out on Tesla's Electric Highway*. [Online]
Available at: https://www.nytimes.com/2013/02/10/automobiles/stalled-on-the-ev-highway.html?ref=automobiles&_r=0
[Accessed August 2021].

Broder, J. M., 2013. *Wheels: That Tesla Data: What It Says and What It Doesn't*. [Online]
Available at: https://wheels.blogs.nytimes.com/2013/02/14/that-tesla-data-what-it-says-and-what-it-doesnt
[Accessed August 2021].

Butterfield, S., 2014. *We Don't Sell Saddles Here. Medium.*. [Online]
Available at: https://medium.com/@stewart/we-dont-sell-saddles-here-4c59524d650d
[Accessed August 2021].

Charity: water, 2021. *Charity: water*. [Online]
Available at: https://www.charitywater.org/
[Accessed July 2021].

Church, M., 2021. *Matt Church*. [Online]
Available at: https://www.mattchurch.com/
[Accessed June 2021].

Collins, D., 2021. *Dan Collins*. [Online]
Available at: https://dancollins.com.au
[Accessed 2021].

Cron, L., 2012. *Wired for story: the writer's guide to using brain science to hook readers from the very first sentence.* New York: Ten Speed Press.

Dimond, A., 2013. *Why Editing Nominations Predict The Best Picture Oscar.* [Online]
Available at: https://variety.com/2013/film/awards/oscars-why-editing-predicts-the-best-picture-1200945193/
[Accessed 2021].

Dolan, G., n.d. *Gabrielle Dolan.* [Online]
Available at: www.gabrielledolan.com
[Accessed 2020].

Dolan, G., n.d. *Gabrielle Dolan.* [Online]
Available at: https://gabrielledolan.com/
[Accessed July 2021].

Fink, C., 2021. *The leverage of speaking.* [Online]
Available at: https://www.colfink.com/articles/the-leverage-of-speaking
[Accessed August 2021].

Gilbert, E., 2009. *Your Elusive Creative Genius.* [Online]
Available at: https://www.ted.com/talks/elizabeth_gilbert_your_elusive_creative_genius
[Accessed 221].

Gilbert, E., 2015. *Big Magic: Creative living beyond fear.* New York: Bloomsbury Publishing.

Gray, D., n.d. *Dave Gray.* [Online]
Available at: http://www.xplaner.com/
[Accessed 2021].

Handley, A., 2014. *Everybody Writes: Your go-to guide to creating ridiculously good content.* Hoboken, NJ: John Wiley & Sons.

Harrison, S., 2018. *Thirst: a story of redemption, compassion, and a mission to bring clean water to the world.* New York: Crown Publishing Group.

Jiwa, B., n.d. *The Story of Telling*. [Online]
Available at: www.thestoryoftelling.com
[Accessed 2021].

John, E., 2019. *Me*. London: MacMillan.

Lamott, A., 1997. *Bird by Bird: Some instructions on writing and life*.
New York: Anchor Books.

Leopold, A., 1968. *A Sand County Almanac*. London: Oxford University
Press.

Levitin, D., 2014. *The Organized Mind: Thinking straight in the age of
information overload*. New York: Dutton.

Merriam-Webster, n.d. *Story*. [Online]
Available at: https://www.merriam-webster.com/dictionary/story
[Accessed 2021].

Mortenson, G., 2006. *Three Cups of Tea*. New York: Penguin.

Musk, E., 2013. *A Most Peculiar Test Drive*. [Online]
Available at: https://www.tesla.com/blog/most-peculiar-test-drive
[Accessed August 2021].

Network for Good, n.d. *How to use storytelling to engage donors*.
[Online]
Available at: https://www.networkforgood.com/resource/how-to-
use-storytelling-to-engage-donors/
[Accessed 2021].

Olson, R., 2015. *Houston, We Have a Narrative: Why science needs
story*. Chicago: University of Chicago Press.

Oxford English Dictionary, n.d. *Connect*. [Online]
Available at: https://www.oed.com/

Pallotta, D., 2013. *TED talk: The Way We Think About Charity is Dead
Wrong*. [Online]
Available at: https://www.ted.com/talks/dan_pallotta_the_way_we_
think_about_charity_is_dead_wrong
[Accessed 2021].

Pressfield, S., 2002. *The War of Art*. New York: Rugged Land.

Rao, S., n.d. *The Unmistakeable Creative Podcast*. [Online]
Available at: https://podcast.unmistakablecreative.com/
[Accessed 2021].

Recode Media, 2021. *Behind the making of The Dissident, the movie about Jamal Khashoggi's murder*. [Online]
Available at: https://podcasts.google.com/feed/aHR0cHM-6Ly9mZWVkcy5tZWdhcGhvbmUuZm0vcmVjb2RlbWVkaWE/
episode/NTUyNWY0MWMtMGQ1Yy0xMWViLTkxNTctOG-ZhYzEyYTJiMGQ3?sa=X&ved=0CAUQkfYCahcKEwils-mdmdzyA-hUAAAAAHQAAAAAQAQ
[Accessed 2021].

Simon, S., 2021. *Amelia Pang's Book Explores the Human Cost of Our Cheap Goods. NPR Morning Edition*. [Online]
Available at: https://www.npr.org/2021/01/30/962358073/amelia-pangs-book-explores-the-human-cost-of-our-cheap-goods
[Accessed 30 January 2021].

Stern, H., 2016. *The Howard Stern Show. SoundCloud.*. [Online]
Available at: https://soundcloud.com/coldplayingpodcast/chris-martin-on-the-howard-stern-show-2016-03-16
[Accessed 2021].

Wardle, D., 2016. *Opening Keynote*. s.l.:The PRSA Counselors Academy 2016 Spring Conference.

Williams, T. T., 2019. *Erosion: Essays of Undoing*. New York: Farrar, Straus and Giroux.

Zander, B. & Zander, R. S., 2002. *The Art of Possibility: Transforming professional and personal life*. London: Penguin Books.

ABOUT THE AUTHOR

Lisa Gerber believes we can all make the world a better place – one story at a time. To that end, she advises purpose-driven leaders on how to make their idea of change happen through effective storytelling and communication. Her training and coaching programs are designed to help organizations get noticed, shift perception, and get funded.

She is the creative behind the renaming of the regional animal welfare organization *Better Together Animal Alliance* and has since been appointed to their Board of Directors. Her work has contributed to the passing of education tax levies and initiatives to fund teacher learning communities and public input gathering for a major cleanup project that increases public access to the waterfront. In 2021, Lisa was appointed Director of Strategy for *Their Story is Our Story: Giving Voice to Refugees*.

When she is not in her office, she might be out skiing or trail running – it's where she does her best creative problem-solving.

She hosts the Breaking Trail podcast, where she uncovers the great stories of outdoor active purpose-driven individuals who are redefining the way they do life and work.

You can follow Lisa's blog at bigleapcreative.com/blog

Contact her at www.bigleapcreative.com

www.ingramcontent.com/pod-product-compliance
Lightning Source LLC
Chambersburg PA
CBHW071422210326
41597CB00020B/3617